THE CASE FOR
DEMOCRATIC
CAPITALISM

Harold W. Chase
University of Minnesota

Paul Dolan
University of Delaware

THOMAS Y. CROWELL COMPANY
New York
Established 1834

To

Helen   Bryce   Eric   Peter   Louise

PREFACE

Too often, we who teach government and economics at the college level assume that students understand either too much or too little about the American governmental and economic systems. When we assume they understand as clearly as we the great strengths of those systems, we may unduly stress shortcomings, hoping that by nurturing the students' critical faculties we will enhance their understanding. When we assume the students come to us fresh from a pap diet of civics-course bromides, the temptation to shock them into thinking may overpower us; and one of the best ways to shock is to attack what they assume, without independent thought on their part, to be the accepted truths about government and economics. The risks attending either alternative are all too apparent: on the one hand, the students may take on an undue and unbecoming cynicism, or, on the other, they may reject outright the instructor's adverse criticisms—both are maladies which inhibit the learning process.

From our own experience, we believe that the best approach to teaching government and economics is to lead the students through an objective analysis without applying a billiards player's English to achieve a teaching effect. If the objective analysis conveys to the students accurate knowledge of, and as a result, a justifiable pride in what we have as Americans, this should be no bar to the development of their critical faculties. Rather, it should provide them a solid basis, in their later studies, for judging more sophisticated interpretations of the strengths and shortcomings of democracy and capitalism. In keeping with these thoughts, we offer the following analysis of the case for democratic capitalism. We do not offer this as a substitute for a basic text or for classroom discussion. It is designed to be interpretive and provocative rather than definitive or exhaustive.

A word about the title. For reasons we explain in the book, we do not feel that a word used to describe a political system is applicable in describing an economic system or vice versa. The word "democratic" is not being used to modify "capitalism," but rather as shorthand for "democratic government." Perhaps a more precise title might have been *The Case for Democratic Government and Capitalism*. But there is a special appeal in the shorter title. For years, American government officials and others have sought an appropriate name to describe the American systems in information-disseminating activities abroad. We believe there is merit in borrowing, as others have done, from those who have long used the term "democratic socialism" to describe the marriage of a democratic governmental system with a socialistic economic system, and to use the word "democratic" in the same way, but pairing it with "capitalism."

Two other matters. First, since in the ensuing discussions the word "democrat" is used extensively, students will perhaps need to be reminded at the outset that democrat with a small d does not mean the same thing as the word capitalized. Second, to keep distracting citations to a minimum, we have not footnoted quotations from well-known sources now in the public domain.

Finally, we should like to express our appreciation to our students, who inspired us to do this book, and to Bernice M. Chase and Philip Winsor, who did so much to put it in publishable form.

Harold W. Chase
New York City

Paul Dolan
Newark, Delaware

CONTENTS

THE PURPOSES OF GOVERNMENT

1.

To facilitate communication and understanding, we would like to define quickly some of the important terms we will be using. Unfortunately, some of the concepts central to discussions of political and economic systems do not have definitions which are universally accepted. Our definitions are not offered as definitive but, rather, only to make clear what we mean. It is important, therefore, in comparing our ideas with the ideas of others, to establish what others mean when they use the words we define now and as we go along.

When we write of *government*, we use it to mean the organization for the direction and control of a people. Among people living together, there are relationships and activities which lie outside the scope of government. For example, among the people of the United States, religious and charitable activities are largely nongovernmental matters. It is useful, therefore, to have another term to describe a people living together. *Community* and *society* are good words for this purpose. The word *state* is useful as a term to encompass the community, its territory, and its government. The relationship of these terms has been succinctly set forth by Professor MacIver:

The state is an association, which acting through law as promulgated by a government endowed to this end with coercive power, maintains within a community territorially demarcated the universal external conditions of social order.[1]

[1] Robert M. MacIver, *The Modern State* (London: Oxford University Press, 1926), p. 22.

In order to make evaluations of particular governmental systems, we must first determine what purposes government is supposed to serve. Toward that end, insights may be gained by attempting to ascertain why societies do have governments. In this connection, it is important to observe that virtually all societies have at all times had some kind of government. True, as described by anthropologists, some of these governments have been very rudimentary. For example, Professor Schapera wrote about the Bergdama and the Bushmen of South Africa:

In effect the affairs of a band are among both peoples managed by its men generally. They forgather every evening round the central camp fire, and as the need arises discuss what should be done. They plan the following day's hunting, and periodically decide upon such other matters as moving camp or burning the veld to stimulate the growth of new plants; among Bergdama they occasionally also plan raids upon nearby Herero cattle-posts, or prohibit food-gathering in localities where the fruits are still green. From time to time they organize initiation ceremonies for boys, among Bergdama they consult with the women about selecting wives for young men, and among Bushmen they occasionally have to decide upon abandoning feeble old people when forced to migrate rapidly. They arrange trading and other visits to friendly neighbours, and take steps to resist aggression or to retaliate against enemies.

In all this, the chief's special function usually is to act as executive officer. He assigns their respective tasks to the hunters, divides the meat of any big game animals that they kill, leads the people and regulates each day's trek whenever they move, sends messengers to other bands and interviews those who come to him, and if not too old takes command on aggressive raids.

He also has certain ritual duties. Among Bergdama these are relatively numerous. He charms hunters to give them success, prepares medicines for use at the boys' initiation ceremonies or by parents who have lost a child, performs rainmaking magic, and in case of misfortune or when the band moves deposits offerings or prays at the grave of a dead ancestor. He also maintains the sacred fire that is held to influence the welfare of his group. This fire, round which the men usually meet, is kept burning continuously under a tree in the centre of the camp. All game killed in the chase, and each kind of berry and tuber as it ripens, is brought there and blessed before being eaten, the old men feed it with scrapings of magical roots while hunters and women are out seeking food, and before the band moves camp or settles in a new home the chief prays at it to the Deity for abundance and good fortune. If times are bad, the diviners may say that it has been polluted and is therefore no longer beneficent; the chief then orders every fire in the camp to be extinguished and with elaborate ceremonial kindles a new one, from which every family takes a brand to start its own again. Only he himself can perform this ritual, or renew the fire should it die accidentally.

In some of these activities he is helped by special assistants. Diviners advise him when to move camp or to perform certain rites. His senior wife tends the sacred fire, and whenever camp is shifted takes along some brands to set it going again; she also performs part of the ritual when hunters are being charmed. The "food-master" sees to the tasting, preparation, and distribution, of all food brought to the fire, accompanies young men who go raiding and performs magic for their success, and "doctors" any hunter who kills a lion.

The only Bushmen among whom the chief is said to have similar duties are the Heikum and Kung. Here he too maintains a sacred fire, at which he ceremonially tastes the meat of big game animals before it is distributed; in early summer he also inaugurates the eating of the new season's plant foods by a special rite in which he prays to the Deity on behalf of his people. Nothing of this kind has been recorded for other Bushmen. But everywhere among them professional magicians also perform rites of communal importance, such as "doctoring" hunters for success, initiating boys into manhood, and making rain. It may be that in such cases they are directed by the chief, but our sources give insufficient detail to determine the question.

The Bergdama or Bushman chief has no legislative or judicial functions, nor are there official tribunals of any other kind. Among Bergdama, it is true, people sometimes ask elderly men to arbitrate their disputes, but such requests are not obligatory nor are the decisions necessarily accepted. Both here and among Bushmen, persons who arouse general hostility, for example by repeated acts of violence or by committing incest, may be punished by thrashing, expulsion from the band, or even death. There seems to be no formal trial; the data indicate merely that the decision to act against the offender is reached casually round the camp fire, and if necessary the younger men are then told to enforce it. Private disputes, on the other hand, are usually settled by self-help. A man who has been robbed or assaulted, whose wife has been seduced, or who has been injured in some other way, avenges himself as best he can, wounding or possibly even killing the culprit, or else resorting to poison or destructive magic. Neither the chief nor anybody else is entitled to intervene, and it is said also that blood vengeance is not practised against someone who thus kills a member of his own band. Similarly, a man may freely thrash or kill a disobedient child or unfaithful wife, or divorce her for any reason by simply sending her away.[2]

---

[2] Isaac Schapera, *Government and Politics in Tribal Societies* (London: C. A. Watts & Co., Ltd., 1956), pp. 85–87.

Among anthropologists and political scientists there are many who feel that such simple political organization cannot be equated to *government*. For them the term *government* defines only those political organizations where there is a substantial degree of coercion and regulation. Nonetheless, in the activities described by Schapera, we can certainly see that there is political organization of a real sort. Rather than quibble over terms, we are willing to admit to a degree of arbitrariness, when we assert that this kind of political organization is government, albeit of a very primitive type.

Assuming that government is universal, the question why it should be so becomes all the more intriguing and meaningful, particularly in light of the fact that most of us yearn for freedom. Who among us has not looked forward to the day when he or she would be free of parental or school authority? Interpolating from our own feelings, we can guess that most people everywhere and at all times yearn for freedom. Why then do we find in virtually all societies at all times governments which limit individual freedom? Does history supply an answer?

THE BEGINNINGS OF GOVERNMENT

Whether or not men ever lived without some kind of government is conjectural. For the sake of logical analysis, some political philosophers like Hobbes and Locke assumed that men first lived in a state of nature, a state of anarchy, and contrived their political arrangements to meet the dangers and inconveniences of this state. They were quick to admit, however, that in actuality there probably never was such a time. Others have theorized that the idea of government evolved from the family. As MacIver has put it: "We cannot cope with the ramifications and vicissitudes of the process in which government became institutionalized, in which the state-form emerged. It is a process that begins before there is any light of history and it is one that is still far from being fulfilled. Under endlessly varied circumstances the 'habits pertaining to government,' which at first were centered in the family and the kin-circle, found a locus in the inclusive community." [3] But, as MacIver indicated, history does not help us much in determining whether or not the *concept* of govern-

---

[3] Robert M. MacIver, *The Web of Government* (New York: The Macmillan Co., 1947), pp. 33–34.

ment was coincident with the birth of man or whether it evolved after man had floundered in something akin to a state of nature. Interestingly enough, we have no mention of political arrangements in Genesis until it is stated that Nimrod became monarch. Today, we are born into some kind of political arrangement just as we are born into a religion. Without thinking much about it, we accept the wisdom and necessity of having government of one form or another. Consequently, even if a large number of us were to embark upon a new life in some remote area as did the Pilgrims of old, it is certain that we would assume that some political arrangements would be necessary and we would make them. Or, if any one of us were to go prospecting for gold alone in some wild uninhabited region, as soon as it became apparent that a large number of other people had come to the same area, he would be quick to decide that it would be wise to have some kind of political organization. Conceivably, the need for organization might be felt after a trying experience living in a state of nature. Actually, it would be impossible to determine whether the early frontier governments were primarily set up because people assumed that they were necessary as a consequence of living under them elsewhere or whether people had to learn the hard way that such arrangements are the only alternative to the insecurities and inconveniences of a state of nature.

The fact that people remain in political arrangements into which they are born without giving the matter much thought should not be interpreted to mean that these arrangements are the consequence of indifference. On the contrary, it may only reflect an awareness that organization is necessary. It is true, of course, that there is constant agitation for change in the particular types of arrangements existing but almost no agitation for doing away with government *per se*, communist dogma about the "withering away of the state" notwithstanding. The real honest-to-goodness anarchist has become as extinct as the proverbial dodo bird.

Despite the fact that we do not know when man first contrived the idea of government, we know a great deal about how some governments were started. There are excellent records of governments which have started from scratch, that is, where a society and government were formed virtually simultaneously. The early American colonies are good examples. You recall from history how the Pilgrims set up their government while afloat, even before setting foot in the new land. Most governments we know about, however, evolved from existing governments or replaced them. In any case, what we know about the history of these governments does not supply us with clues as to what human needs gave rise originally to the institution of government. By the time these governments were formed, the idea that some form of government is necessary for a society was accepted as a matter of course.

DEDUCING THE PURPOSES

Since there is no way to establish empirically the reasons why mankind has decided, or accepted the fact, that government is necessary or desirable, or both, we can only theorize about them. This we shall proceed to do, borrowing heavily from some who have theorized before us. In doing so, we shall not attempt to reconstruct the actual process by which government came about. We feel it would be more fruitful to seek to deduce the reasons why the idea of government has appealed to and continues to appeal to the members of any society at any time.

Protection

Several centuries ago, the political theorist Thomas Hobbes suggested that the best way to determine the purpose of government was to picture what life would be like without it. He conjured up this picture:

Whatsoever therefore is consequent to a time of Warre, where every man is Enemy to every man; the same is consequent to the time, wherein men live without other security than what their own strength, and their own invention shall furnish them withall. In such condition, there is no place for Industry, because the fruit thereof is uncertain: and consequently no Culture of the Earth; no Navigation, nor use of the commodities that may be imported by Sea; no commodious Buildings; no Instruments of moving, and removing, such things as require much force; no Knowledge of the face of the Earth; no account of Time; no Arts; no Letters; no Society; and, which is worst of all, continuall feare, and danger of violent death; And the life of man, solitary, poore, nasty, brutish, and short.

To those who argued that Hobbes' view of human nature was too pessimistic, Hobbes' answer was:

It may seem strange to some man that has not well weighted these things; that Nature should thus disassociate, and render men apt to invade and destroy one another; and he may therefore, not trusting to this Inference, made from the Passions, desire perhaps to have the same confirmed by Experience. Let him therefore consider with himselfe: when taking a journey, he armes himselfe, and seeks to go well accompanied; when going to sleep, he locks his dores; when even in his house he locks his chests; and this when he knowes there bee Lawes, and publike Officers, armed, to revenge all injuries shall bee done him; what opinion he has of his fellow-subjects, when he rides armed; of his fellow Citizens, when he locks his dores; and of his children and servants, when he locks his chests. Does he not there as much accuse mankind by his actions, as I do by my words?

As distasteful and overdrawn as the Hobbesian view of human nature may be, experience indicates that in the main it is realistic. Would you be willing to live in a community where it was every man for himself?

Whether or not the Hobbesian view is valid in terms of actual experience, we should recognize, in establishing the purposes of government, that people from time immemorial have generally accepted it as valid. To illustrate, even scripture supports the Hobbesian view. It is written in Genesis that after the Flood, "the Lord said in his heart, I will not again curse the ground any more for man's sake; for the imagination of man's heart is evil from his youth." And Paul warns in his Second Epistle to Timothy that even "in the last days perilous times shall come. For men shall be lovers of their own selves, covetous, boasters, proud, blasphemers, disobedient to parents, unthankful, unholy, without natural affection, truce-breakers, false accusers, incontinent, fierce, despisers of those that are good, traitors, heady, highminded, lovers of pleasures more than lovers of God. . . ."

The Father of our Constitution, James Madison, made it clear that he and presumably the others at the Constitutional Convention took a generally Hobbesian view of the nature of man. In explaining why it was necessary to seek devices to provide checks on those who would govern the society, Madison wrote in *The Federalist:*

It may be a reflection on human nature, that such devices [checks and balances] should be necessary to control the abuses of government. But what is government itself, but the greatest of all reflections on human nature? If men were angels, no government would be necessary. If angels were to govern men, neither external nor internal controls on government would be necessary. In framing a government which is to be administered by men over men, the great difficulty lies in this; you must first enable the government to control the governed; and in the next place oblige it to control itself. A dependence on the people is, no doubt, the primary control on the government; but experience has taught mankind the necessity of auxiliary precautions.

Does recent study and research by psychologists substantiate or invalidate this assessment of human nature? Professor Abraham H. Maslow, the Chairman of the Psychology Department at Brandeis University, has supplied a good answer to that question. In a work in which he espoused an optimistic view of human nature, he wrote:

"Evil" behavior has mostly referred to unwarranted hostility, cruelty, destructiveness, "mean" aggressiveness. This we do not know enough about. To the degree that this quality of hostility is instinctoid, mankind has one kind of future. To the degree that it is reactive (a response to bad treatment), mankind has a very different kind of future. My opinion is that the weight of evidence so far indicates that indiscriminately *destructive* hostility is reactive, because uncovering therapy reduces it, and changes its quality into "healthy" self-affirmation, forcefulness, selective hostility, self-defense, righteous indignation, etc. In any case, the *ability* to be aggressive and angry is found in all self-actualizing people, who are able to let it flow freely when the external situation "calls for" it.

. . . . . .

Evil behaviors seem to most psychologists to be reactive . . . rather than instinctive. This implies that "bad" behavior is very deeply rooted in human nature and can never be abolished altogether, it may yet be expected to lessen as the personality matures and as the society improves.[4]

In short, Maslow suggested that, on the basis of available study and research, there is good reason to believe that personality development and improvement of the environment can *moderate* "evil" behavior. But note carefully his admission that " 'bad' behavior is very deeply rooted in human nature and can never be abolished altogether." Note, also, that Maslow measured his words carefully when he wrote of the possibility of moderating "evil" behavior. He said "it may be expected." The implication is clear—there is no satisfactory example from human experience to demonstrate that personality

---

[4] Abraham H. Maslow, *Toward a Psychology of Being* (Princeton: D. Van Nostrand Co., Inc., 1962), pp. 182–83.

THE PURPOSES OF GOVERNMENT / 9

development and improvement of the environment *have* done so.

Paradoxically, in view of the marked distrust of their peoples manifested by communist governments, one of the implied tenets of communism is that men are capable, at least ultimately, of comporting themselves like angels. Marxist doctrine calls for men to give according to their abilities and to receive according to their needs. Under such a scheme, men would be expected to be altruistic enough to work to the utmost of their ability without regard to rewards. But this notion denies the lessons of history. Men may not live by bread alone, but few are so unselfish as to give of themselves constantly without regard to what others contribute and the rewards they receive. This is attested to by the fact that the many utopian societies established on the basis of men giving according to their abilities and receiving according to their needs were short-lived in their original forms.[5] It is also instructive to reflect on the Russian communists' experience with incentive systems of remuneration for working people. When the communists took control of the government of Russia, incentive rate systems of remuneration were rejected as capitalistic devices aimed at exploiting workers. To pay people on the basis of how well they produced is, of course, contrary to the idea of giving according to ability and taking according to needs. People should and, in the utopian communistic state, so it was thought, would be willing to give according to their ability without regard to rewards. The communist leaders discovered that Russians were human beings too. Individual production in factories dropped to such an alarming extent that it became imperative to set up incentive systems of pay once again in order to raise the levels of production to levels commensurate with similar plants in capitalistic countries.

Nevertheless, undaunted by this experience, the Russian communist leaders have continued to profess their belief in the doctrine. As late as 1961, in the Party's draft program, they promised: "All sources of public wealth will gush forth abundantly, and the great principle 'from each according to his ability, to each according to his needs' will be implemented." But, significantly, they fixed the time for it to happen some years off: "In the next decade (1971–1980) the material and technical basis of communism will be created

---

[5] See article on "Communistic Settlements" in the *Encyclopaedia of the Social Sciences* (New York: The Macmillan Co., 1931). Also, see "Spirit of Kibbutz Fading in Israel," *The New York Times*, June 18, 1961.

 **WHY SOVIET INDUSTRY IS SHORT OF MANPOWER**

	RUSSIA	U.S.
Russia's labor force outnumbers that of U.S.	109.6 MILLION	72.3 MILLION
BUT: Russia, with inefficient farming methods, uses nearly 10 times as many people as the U.S. to do farm work.	52.0 MILLION	5.8 MILLION
Russia also has larger armed forces	3.6 MILLION	2.5 MILLION
RESULT: Russia has fewer workers for industries, trades, services, other types of work.	54.0 MILLION	64.0 MILLION

Reprinted from *U.S. News & World Report,* May 2, 1960, published at Washington. Copyright 1960, U.S. News & World Report, Inc.

and there will be an abundance of material and cultural benefits for the whole population. Soviet society *will come close* to a stage where it can introduce the principle of distribution according to needs" (italics supplied). This statement invites the cynical observation that the leaders are allowing themselves plenty of time to deliver on their promises as well as a way out if they cannot. In this connection, it is worth noting that in 1958, Khrushchev told Senator Humphrey: "You know . . . what those [Chinese] communes are based on? They are based on that principle, 'From each according to his abilities, to each according to his needs.' You know that won't work. You can't get production without incentive." [6] The newspaper accounts on the next few pages provide an interesting commentary on this point.

Too, communists for years have talked about the withering away of the state. They have argued that after people were freed from their capitalistic oppressors and learned to take care of themselves there would be no need for government in the usual sense because man is inherently good. Obviously, this concept is contrary to Madison's. But again, historical experience demonstrates how unrealistic such an approach is. In the Soviet Union the state has not withered away. On the contrary, it has become more pervasive in the lives of its people. For a time Soviet leaders soft-pedaled the withering away of the state theme as it became apparent that they had no intention of abdicating their power. The new tack is that only the aggressive designs of the capitalists prevent the withering away.

[6] Editorial, *The Minneapolis Sunday Tribune,* March 11, 1962.

Russian Attacks
Equal-Pay Trend

Official Says Salaries Must Reflect Skill and Output

By THEODORE SHABAD
Special to The New York Times

MOSCOW, April 4—The Soviet Government warned today against indiscriminate use of collective payment systems that tend to level wages. Such systems appear to be spreading in the country's economy.

A long article in Pravda, the Communist party newspaper, said that collective payment, in which wages are distributed evenly among workers of production teams, amounted to a leveling of wages "that is inadmissible in Communist construction."

The writer of the article, Aleksandr P. Volkov, who is chairman of the State Labor and Wage Committee, declared that only certain kinds of occupations were suitable for collective payment systems based on piece work.

He listed team operations such as mining, building, assembly-line work and team servicing of large equipment and machines in the steel and chemical industries.

Pay Must Reflect Skill

However, even in such collective operations, Mr. Volkov added, it would be wrong to distribute pay evenly among team members. Each worker must be paid according to his skills and his contributions to the end product, he added.

Recent pronouncements by Soviet Government and party officials have consistently emphasized the need for material incentives to increase production. The Pravda article appeared to be expressing concern that some industries, by adopting collective payment systems, were departing from the incentive principle.

Mr. Volkov said that individual piece-work payments would continue to be "the most effective system" in most machine-tool operations, in the textile industries and in other occupations "where the worker is responsible for an unlimited number of machines."

The Soviet official criticized recent writings by economists who had sought to discredit individual payment systems. One writer, A. Mandrugin, was taken to task for having called for the abolition of what he termed "the existing system of excessive personal incentives in the form of individual piece-work payments."

Piece-Work Defended

Mr. Volkov denied that such piece-work systems were "in serious contradiction to the development of our society or allegedly promote individualism and weaken the strength of the collective."

Mr. Mandrugin had made this charge in an article published in the economic newspaper Ekonomicheskaya Gazeta.

Mr. Volkov also called for a revision of work norms. When workers produce in excess of such norms they receive premium payments. The wage chairman said the norms were often placed too low and thus failed to stimulate labor productivity or increases in workers' skills.

He attributed an excessive labor turnover in some areas to the fact that workers prefered employment in factories that set low norms, thus making it easier to overfulfill plans and earn higher pay.

In 1957, in a speech marking the anniversary of the Bolshevik Revolution, Khrushchev said:

Communes Naive, Moscow Charges

It Denies Communism Can Be Speeded by the Method Employed by Peiping

By SEYMOUR TOPPING
Special to The New York Times

MOSCOW, Nov. 12—The Soviet Communist Party denounced today as "naively romantic" the theory that a Socialist state could hasten its transition to communism through the organization of communes.

The Soviet party avoided direct criticism of the commune system in Communist China. It restricted itself to citing the failure of its own minor experiments immediately after the Bolshevik revolution. The implications were clear, nevertheless.

The Kremlin's position was stated in an article contributed by the Soviet party to the current issue of Problems of Peace and Socialism, organ of the Communist and Workers parties published in Prague. It was entitled "The Main Link of Transition to Communism."

Parley in Its Third Day

The article took on special significance because of the current meeting here between Premier Khrushchev and Liu Shaochi, Chairman of the Chinese People's Republic, and other leading figures of the Communist world. The closed conference, now in its third day in the Kremlin, is said to be discussing ideological differences within the Communist bloc.

The article in Problems of Peace and Socialism indicated how deepseated these differences are in the economic as well as the political spheres. Mr. Khrushchev's thesis that world communism must be achieved in the course of "peaceful coexistence" rather than through war is also being examined at the conference.

The article said the Soviet party was struggling to defend "its correct and scientific understanding of the essence of communism against different kinds of vulgar conceptions."

It said that one of these "incorrect and vulgar conceptions" was an attempt to put all of society on the same economic level immediately through a system of communes. The article contended that this theory failed to appreciate the incentive value of graduated wages.

Stress On Distribution

Supporters of the commune theory were criticized for putting emphasis on problems of distribution rather than on building communism through "the creation of a mighty material, technical base."

Recalling the failure of Soviet experiments in 1918–19 with forms of agricultural, village and town communes in which wages were put into a "common pot," the article stated:

"This expressed, narrow tendency to consumption was based on inadequate development of productive forces and limited quantities of consumer goods. These ideas minimized the role of material incentives in increasing the skills and productivity of labor."

The article said this attempt to "leap forward" across unfinished stages of development always caused negative and painful reactions. It added:

"The Communist party of the Soviet Union applied serious criticism to these opinions, which were sometimes naïvely romantic or sometimes born because resources were limited. They were always mistaken and this form of distribution died away."

Soviet Has Master Plan

The article noted that the desire to level out society "still is sometimes resurrected among some Soviet people even now."

The controversy dwelt upon in the article was regarded by Western experts as not simply an ideological one. It relates directly to Moscow's efforts to organize the pattern of economic development in Communist countries according to a master plan.

Much of the Kremlin's international economic planning is channeled through its economic organization for Eastern Europe. Red China and the other Communist nations of Asia are represented only as observers.

The Kremlin's efforts to integrate Chinese economic development into that of Eastern Europe, with specific areas of industrial specialization, hinges to a large extent on the Soviet program of economic and technical assistance to Peiping.

Sharp Criticism Noted

The article in Problems of Peace and Socialism disclosed frankly the extent to which Moscow's theories had come under attack.

"Revisionists and opportunists of all colors have spread different kinds of insinuations affirming that the Communist party of the Soviet Union allegedly is very careless on questions of theory and assumes an attitude of narrow practicism," the article said. "It is obvious that these affirmations are untruthful and have no basis.

"There would be no sense in denying them except that it is not only a question of slander but also that the authors of such affirmations do not understand, or consciously distort, the whole process of development of Marxist-Leninist theory in general, and in the modern epoch particularly."

The article charged that critics of the Soviet party were "playing with abstract dialectical conceptions" and failing to apply Marxist-Leninist theory to the problems of life.

The smaller the threat of an attack from outside, the less efforts and means will we expend on this function [defense] of our state.

The Marxist-Lenin teaching on the state, on its dying off in proportion to the movement of society toward complete communism, is of enormous significance.

From the point of view of the internal development of the Soviet Union, it would be quite possible and very expedient to transfer the great expenditures for the defense of the country, for the upkeep of the state organs linked with the defense of socialism from hostile forces and their agents, to a still greater development of economy, for raising the level of the people's living standard.

For our discussion, the significant point is that there has been no withering away of the state nor is there likely ever to be.

Nor have communists been the only ones to take an unduly optimistic view of human nature. Many democrats in the last few centuries have been beguiled by the idea of the perfectability of man. Reinhold Niebuhr, one of the great theologians and political philosophers of our time has put it this way: "Our modern civilization . . . was ushered in on a wave of boundless social optimism.

"Great News — In Another 20 Years We May Get Some Of The Things We Expected 30 Years Ago"

Herblock in *The Washington Post*, August 1, 1961.

Modern secularism is divided into many schools. But all the various schools agreed in rejecting the Christian doctrine of original sin." [7] And he went on to indicate the fallacy of such thinking:

---

[7] Reinhold Niebuhr, *The Children of Light and the Children of Darkness* (New York: Charles Scribner's Sons, 1944), pp. 16–17.

But it is necessary to point out that the doctrine [of original sin] makes an important contribution to any adequate social and political theory the lack of which has robbed bourgeois theory of real wisdom; for it emphasizes a fact which every page of human history attests. Through it one may understand that no matter how wide the perspectives which the human mind may reach, how broad the loyalties which the human imagination may conceive, how universal the community which human statecraft may organize or how pure the aspirations of the saintliest idealists may be, there is no level of human moral or social achievement in which there is not some corruption of inordinate self-love.

As we understand it, Niebuhr is here not thinking of "original sin" in the sense that men are born in sin and incapable of modifying their natures, but rather in the sense that however successful some men are in improving themselves, there will always be "some corruption of inordinate self-love."

It is also significant to note that British Fabian socialists for years argued that once there was a Labour Government in Britain there would never be a labor strike against the government because the government and the unions would have the public good at heart. Much to the surprise and chagrin of Britain's Labour Government after the war, unions pursuing their own self-interest chose to strike against the government when they did not get their way, irrespective of the public good.

A realistic appraisal of human nature should not induce despair. Such an appraisal does not compel the belief that all people are bad all of the time, and that hope for any kind of decent life in a society is vain. We know pragmatically that people can learn to live together provided their institutions are based on a realistic understanding of human strengths and failings. This idea will be developed more fully in the discussion of democracy in another chapter. For now, it is worth reflecting on these thoughts. Which marriage stands the better chance for success, the one where both partners assume and expect their spouses to be angels or the one in which each partner understands the strengths and weaknesses in the character of the other? Parenthetically, just as husbands and wives can love their mates in spite of their weaknesses, so people understanding full well the weaknesses and strengths of mankind can have love and compassion for their fellow men.

To sum up, it seems a valid deduction that one of the chief reasons the idea of government has universal appeal is that men see in it a means for protecting themselves from one another. Because self-preservation is one of the most powerful of human motivations, that appeal must be exceedingly strong. Nor would it alter the past or present appeal if we were to concede the possibility that at some future time man might achieve perfection. Until the millennium is reached, the desire for protection will be ever present.

"Convenience"

The great political theorist John Locke many years ago supplied us with another reason for the appeal of the idea of government. He pointed out that where people live in a "state of nature," there is the "inconvenience" of not having a systematic and just way of settling disputes which are bound to arise when people live in close proximity to one another:

. . . I doubt not but it will be objected, that it is unreasonable for men to be judges in their own cases, that self-love will make men partial to themselves and their friends: and, on the other side, that ill-nature, passion, and revenge will carry them too far in punishing others; and hence nothing but confusion and disorder will follow: and that therefore God hath certainly appointed government to restrain the partiality and violence of men. I easily grant, that civil government is the proper remedy for the inconveniencies of the state of nature, which must certainly be great, where men may be judges in their own case; since it is easy to be imagined, that he who was so unjust as to do his brother an injury, will scarce be so just as to condemn himself for it. . . .

Expanding on Locke's idea, there are a legion of other kinds of inconveniences which would confront a heavily-populated society which had no government. How would traffic be regulated? How, indeed, would the whole host of services which are carried on by modern governments be performed? As one reflects on that question, the idea that a modern society, even if it were composed of angels, could do without government seems ludicrous.

Development of the Individual

There is a third basic reason for the necessity of government. Presumably, even in this crowded world of ours, people have the option of withdrawing from the society of others. To what extent the remote areas of the earth could accommodate large numbers of people who wanted to be alone is conjectural. Nonetheless, there are few Henry Thoreaus who prefer solitude at isolated Walden Ponds to living with other people. Man has frequently been described as a social animal. For the vast majority of us, however much we may yearn at times for temporary refuge from society, retreating from the society of other people forever is unthinkable. In this connection, however, it is important to note that most psychologists would reject the idea that people are *born* with a strong motivation to associate with others, to be gregarious. After assessing the evidence on the subject of "gregariousness," social psychologist Otto Klineberg concluded that "it has a possible though doubtful continuity with the behavior of animals; it has no known physiological or anatomical foundation; it is universal in a minimum form but this minimum can probably be adequately explained on the basis of family relationships. The extensions beyond this are determined by practical considerations." [8] Klineberg did not deny that we have the need; rather, he made it clear that those of us who have it have acquired it, presumably by learning that we prefer living in a society to solitude. How we come by the need does not alter the fact that once the need exists it becomes a factor in creating an appeal for the idea of government. Evidently, for fulfillment, the human spirit requires something more than mere gratification of physical needs. Once man becomes aware of spiritual and intellectual needs, he learns that he can meet them best in company with others. He also learns that government can be an agency for helping him meet some of them, for example, by establishing and maintaining an educational system. As man learns that government can be used in this way, he learns that government can be a helpful agency to enable him to better meet his physical needs. By providing some organization, direction, and regulation of the economy, government can enable a society to be more productive materially and provide a better standard of living for its members.

SUMMARY

Although men everywhere can and do advocate further and more specific purposes for government than those dealt with above, it is not likely that they could win *universal* assent for them. It is our contention that there is already such assent for the purposes ex-

---

[8] Otto Klineberg, *Social Psychology* (New York: Holt, Rinehart and Winston, Inc., 1954), p. 160.

plained here. We feel, therefore, that these are the basic minimum purposes, which make a sort of common denominator by which to test the performance of various forms of government. In this connection, several additional points must be made. First, it is undoubtedly true that some see government as an agency by which they can control or dominate a society to fulfill their own needs and gratify their own selfish interests. But such a view is so patently a perversion of the legitimate purposes of government that we need not dwell on it. Unfortunately, however, it is usually the case that those who hold such a view dress their real feelings in more acceptable attire by asserting that they are exercising the powers of government to achieve purposes which are more palatable to the society. For this reason, it is necessary to distinguish carefully between what those who govern profess and what they really desire, and often this is not easy to do.

Second, in assaying how a particular form of government fulfills the purposes which have the assent of all mankind, we must bear in mind that government can itself be an enemy to these purposes rather than a force for achieving them. For example, the evil aspects of the human nature of the governors can threaten individual members of a society just as surely as they are threatened by each other, perhaps more so. Wasn't this precisely what Madison suggested in the quotation cited earlier when he wrote: "In framing a government which is to be administered by men over men, the great difficulty lies in this; you must first enable the government to control the governed; and in the next place oblige it *to control itself*" (italics supplied). Not only may government jeopardize the safety of members of the society; it may also create "inconveniences" and inhibit the strivings of individuals for spiritual, intellectual, and material fulfillment.

SELECTED BIBLIOGRAPHY

HADLEY CANTRIL, *Human Nature and Political Systems* (New Brunswick: Rutgers University Press, 1961).

THOMAS HOBBES, *Leviathan* (There are many editions of this work, at least one of which will be found in most libraries).

JOHN LOCKE, *Second Treatise on Civil Government* (There are many editions of this work, at least one of which will be found in most libraries).

ROBERT M. MACIVER, *The Web of Government* (New York: The Macmillan Co., 1947).

ABRAHAM H. MASLOW, *Toward a Psychology of Being* (Princeton: D. Van Nostrand Co., Inc., 1962).

REINHOLD NIEBUHR, *The Children of Light and the Children of Darkness* (New York: Charles Scribner's Sons, 1944).

JEAN-JACQUES ROUSSEAU, *The Social Contract* (There are many editions of this work, at least one of which will be found in most libraries).

ISAAC SCHAPERA, *Government and Politics in Tribal Societies* (London: C. A. Watts & Co., Ltd., 1956).

GRAHAM WALLAS, *Human Nature in Politics* (New York: Alfred A. Knopf, Inc., 3rd ed., 1921).

THE FORMS OF GOVERNMENT:
DEMOCRATIC vs. AUTHORITARIAN

2.

Government takes a wide variety of forms as befits a creation of men's minds. Classification of these forms is easy yet difficult. All governments can be classified for general purposes under a few headings. Centuries ago, Plato classified governments as aristocracies, oligarchies, democracies, or tyrannies. Since then writers have contrived different classifications or given Plato's classifications different names, but rarely have governments been classified under more than a few general headings for analytical purposes. In our present bi-polar world it seems fitting to use only two classifications, democracy and authoritarianism. Roughly, democracy describes those governments in which the people as a whole, directly or indirectly, hold the ultimate power; and those governments where an elite have asserted and exercise the ultimate power are authoritarian. To classify all governments under these two headings means, of course, that each will contain a rich variety of forms. Too, there will be a matter of degree to consider. In this context, a particular government classified as a democracy will be more or less democratic than others; a particular government classified as authoritarian will be more or less authoritarian than others.

Another problem which arises in this dichotomous classification of governments is that some governments have characteristics of both forms in such degree as to make it difficult to assign them to one category or the other. This is particularly true where the actual operation of government differs from what it is supposed to be in theory.

What we have in mind here is the situation where a government of a society may actually be a dictatorship even though the constitution under which the government is supposed to operate calls for democratic institutions. However, despite the difficulties, the democratic-authoritarian classification seems to us valid and useful for purposes of analyzing the major nation-governments of our age.

DEMOCRACY

Just for the fun of it and to prove a point, ask ten American adults picked at random to define what they mean by the word "democracy." More than likely, you will get ten answers substantively different from each other. It is a strange and sad commentary that, although we proudly regard ourselves as citizens of a great democracy, there is little agreement or understanding about what we mean by the word "democracy." This was not always the case. In ancient times "democracy" had a very precise meaning. The word was derived from two Greek words which put together meant "government by the people." It was used to describe a form of government in which all members of the society (except those who then were considered as less than persons, i.e., slaves, women, and children) participated directly and equally in open meetings where the important governmental decisions were made. However, it is obvious, of course, that in a far more populous society such as we know today it would be impractical to have all citizens participate directly. As Rousseau wrote: "If we take the term in its strict meaning, no true democracy has ever existed, nor ever will. It is against the natural order that a large number should rule and a small number be ruled. It is inconceivable that the People should be in permanent session for the administration of public affairs, and it is clear that commissions could not be set up for that purpose without the form of the administration being thereby changed."

Democracy, therefore, came in time to mean a government in which the ultimate power, the sovereignty, resided in the people as a whole and was to be exercised by their elected representatives for set periods of time, such periods to be relatively short, from one to six years. Were representatives elected for longer periods, it would be difficult for the people to exercise any control over them.

CONFUSION AS TO
FORM, ESSENCE, AND IDEAL

In seeking to set up a new government for a society, it is a mark of wisdom for the framers to ask, "What are we trying to achieve?" After answering this question, the Framers can then go on to ask, "What kind of government will best achieve these ends?" The framers of our government answered the first question in the pre-amble to the Federal Constitution. "We the People of the United States, in Order to form a more perfect Union, establish Justice, insure domestic Tranquility, provide for the common defense, pro-mote the general Welfare, and Secure the Blessings of Liberty to ourselves and our Posterity, do ordain and establish this Constitution for the United States of America." In the process of writing the Constitution, they made it clear that they did not feel that these objectives could be achieved by what at that time was defined as democratic government. For example, John Randolph of Virginia in the opening speech of the Convention said: "Our chief danger arises from the democratic parts of our [State] constitutions. It is a maxim which I hold incontrovertible, that the powers of government exer-cised by the people swallow up the other branches." Later Alexander Hamilton pointedly stated:

All communities divide themselves into the few and the many. The first are the rich and well born, the other the mass of the people. The voice of the people has been said to be the voice of God; and however gen-erally this maxim has been quoted and believed, it is not true in fact. The people are turbulent and changing; they seldom judge or determine right. Give therefore to the first class a distinct, permanent share in the government. They will check the unsteadiness of the second, and as they cannot receive any advantage by a change, they will ever maintain good government. Can a democratic assembly who annually revolve in the mass of people, be supposed steadily to pursue the public good? Nothing but a permanent body can check the imprudence of democracy.

The more moderate "Father of the Constitution," James Madi-son, said:

The government we mean to erect is intended to last for ages. The landed interest, at present, is prevalent; but in the process of time when we approximate to the states and kingdoms of Europe; when the number of landholders shall be comparatively small, through the various means of trade and manufactures, will not the landed interests be overbalanced in future elections, and unless wisely provided against, what will become of your government? In England, at this day, if elections were open to all classes of people, the property of the landed proprietors would be insecure. An agrarian law would soon take place. If these observations be just, our government ought to secure the permanent interests of the country against innovation.

Our Founding Fathers came by their distrust of democracy honestly. They believed along with Madison that men were less than angels, and feared, therefore, that in a democratic society a majority would oppress the minority. Madison expressed this fear in *The Federalist, Number 10:*

From this view of the subject it may be concluded that a pure democracy, by which I mean a society consisting of a small number of citizens, who assemble and administer the government in person, can admit of no cure for the mischiefs of faction. A common passion or interest will, in almost every case, be felt by a majority of the whole; a communication and concert result from the form of government itself; and there is nothing to check the inducements to sacrifice the weaker party or an obnoxious individual. Hence, it is that such democracies have ever been spectacles of turbulence and contention; have ever been found incompatible with personal security or the rights of property; and have in general been as short in their lives as they have been violent in their deaths. Theoretic politicians, who have patronized this species of government, have erroneously supposed that by reducing mankind to a perfect equality in their political rights, they would at the same time, be perfectly equalized and assimilated in their possessions, their opinions, and their passions.

The Founding Fathers were very familiar with the writings of the great political philosophers who preceded them. Democracy as a form of government had not generally found favor in the thinking of these men. Even Locke, who asserted that the sovereignty of the commonwealth resides in the people and who provided a good rationale for democracy, preferred that the English retain their monarchy.

The Framers' view of history both ancient and modern was, perhaps, for them the most telling indictment against democracy. For a short time, at the outset of the Revolution, the ideas which had whipped up enthusiasm for the battle for independence, like "no taxation without representation," had a very real impact on American leaders who consequently at that time were more favorably disposed to democracy. This was demonstrated by the unequivocal words of the Declaration of Independence:

We hold these truths to be self-evident, that all men are created equal, that they are endowed by their Creator with certain unalienable Rights, that among these are Life, Liberty, and the pursuit of Happiness. That to secure these rights, Governments are instituted among Men, deriving their just powers from the consent of the governed.

But postwar events did much to disenchant American leaders with government by the people. In Massachusetts, the farmers of western Massachusetts forcibly closed the courts to prevent the collection of debts. In Rhode Island, where agrarians dominated the legislature, there was a marked tendency for the lawmakers to inflate the currency and favor debtors. To the solid citizens who took the lead in the Constitutional Convention in 1787, these acts were conclusive evidence that rule by a majority of the people would be irresponsible and destructive of individual and property rights. As Madison indicated:

Among the numerous advantages promised by a well-constructed Union, none deserves to be more accurately developed than its tendency to break and control the violence of faction. The friend of popular governments never finds himself so much alarmed for their character and fate, as when he contemplates their propensity to this dangerous vice. He will not fail, therefore, to set a due value on any plan which, without violating the principles to which he is attached, provides a proper cure for it. The instability, injustice, and confusion introduced into the public councils, have, in truth, been the mortal diseases under which popular governments have everywhere perished; as they continue to be the favorite and fruitful topics from which the adversaries to liberty derive their most-specious declamations. The valuable improvements made by the American constitutions [state] on the popular models, both ancient and modern, cannot certainly be too much admired; but it would be an unwarrantable partiality, to contend that they have as effectually obviated the danger on this side, as was wished and expected. Complaints are everywhere heard from our most considerate and virtuous citizens, equally the friends of public and private faith, and of public and personal liberty, that our governments are too unstable, that the public good is disregarded in the conflicts of rival parties, and that measures are too often decided, not according to the rules of justice and the rights of the minor party, but by the superior force of an interested and overbearing majority. However anxiously we may wish that these complaints had no foundation, the evidence of known facts will not permit us to deny that they are in some degree true. It will be found, indeed, on a candid review of our situation, that some of the distresses under which we labour have been erroneously charged on the operation of our governments; but it will be found, at the same time, that other causes will not alone account for many of our heaviest misfortunes; and, particularly, for that prevailing and increasing distrust of public engagements, and alarm for private rights, which are echoed from one end of the continent to the other. These must be chiefly, if not wholly, effects of the unsteadiness and injustice with which a factious spirit has tainted our public administrations.

In short, as Madison saw it, the troubles that were besetting the states resulted not from too little democracy but rather from too much.

But just as the framers distrusted democracy, they also distrusted rule by an elite. After all, if men were not angels, how could they expect a small group of men to exercise absolute power any more impartially than a majority? Consequently, they settled on a mixed government, one in which the majority and the elite would serve as a check on each other. They called it a *republican* form of government.

The Senate was established, in part, as a check on the House of Representatives. Originally, our senators were chosen by the state legislatures rather than by the voters at large. Further, the Senate was and is still not representative. Little Delaware has as many senators as the most populous states. The senators are in office for a term of six years as opposed to the two-year term of Representatives. There is no mystery as to why the Senate was so composed. It was explained in *The Federalist:*

The necessity of a senate is not less indicated by the propensity of all single and numerous assemblies to yield to the impulse of sudden and violent passions, and to be seduced by factious leaders into intemperate and pernicious resolutions. Examples on this subject might be cited without number; and from proceedings within the United States, as well as from the history of other nations. But a position that will not be contradicted, need not be proved. All that need be remarked is, that a body which is to correct this infirmity ought itself to be free from it, and consequently ought to be less numerous. It ought, moreover, to possess great firmness, and consequently ought to hold its authority by a tenure of considerable duration.

Not only did the Framers intend to check popular government by establishing a bicameral legislature, but also they hoped to achieve more of the same by setting up a strong, independent President. Our President, unlike the British Prime Minister, is not dependent upon the legislature for his tenure of office except in the aggravated case where he may be subject to impeachment. In the beginning, the President was elected by a very special process which did not permit the general electorate to participate directly. The electoral college, of course, is still part and parcel of the system but it has been modified to allow for more participation by all citizens. The President has the power to veto legislation. Hamilton explained the President's role vis-à-vis the legislature in this way:

There are some who would be inclined to regard the servile pliancy of the executive to a prevailing current, either in the community or in the legislature, as its best recommendation. But such men entertain very crude notions, as well of the purposes for which government was instituted, as of the true means by which the public happiness may be promoted. The republican principle demands that the deliberate sense of the community should govern the conduct of those to whom they intrust the management of their affairs; but it does not require an unqualified complaisance to every sudden breeze of passion, or to every transient impulse which the people may receive from the arts of men, who flatter their prejudices to betray their interest. It is a just observation, that the people commonly *intend* the PUBLIC GOOD. This often applies to their very errors. But their good sense would despise the adulator who should pretend that they always *reason right* about the *means* of promoting it. They know from experience that they sometimes err; and the wonder is that they so seldom err as they do, beset, as they continually are, by the wiles of parasites and sycophants, by the snares of the ambitious, the avaricious, the desperate, by the artifices of men who possess their confidence more than they deserve it; and of those who seek to possess, rather than to deserve it. When occasions present themselves, in which the interests of the people are at variance with their inclinations, it is the duty of the persons whom they have appointed, to be the guardians of those interests; to withstand the temporary delusion, in order to give them time and opportunity for more cool and sedate reflection. Instances might be cited, in which a conduct of this kind has saved the people from very fatal consequences of their own mistakes, and has procured lasting monuments of their gratitude to the men who had courage and magnanimity enough to serve them at the peril of their displeasure.

In short, the Presidency was looked upon as a brake on hasty legislative action.

There is still good and spirited debate whether or not the Framers *intended* that the Supreme Court have the power to review acts of Congress. The Constitution and the proceedings attendant to the framing of the document are not conclusive on this point. In any case, John Marshall did effectively assert such power for the Court and Alexander Hamilton for one felt the Constitution provided that it be exercised. Judicial review however desirable is in essence undemocratic.

In addition to these checks on popular government, the Framers added a host of others, making the Constitution the supreme law of the land and then making it difficult to amend, forbidding the state and national legislatures to perform specific kinds of acts such as "impairing the obligation of contracts."

Although one may make a case to show that for their time the Founding Fathers were more democratically inclined than most of the world's political leaders, the instrument which they created does not establish a democratic government in the classical sense. The Framers would have been the first to admit it. Moreover, they would have argued that classical democracy was a poor way to achieve the ends of the state which they contemplated.

As one might expect, the Framers themselves dominated the early government under the Constitution. They steered a steady course between what they considered the Scylla of democratic government and the Charybdis of monarchical government. But throughout the land protagonists for democratic government were coming to the fore. Thomas Jefferson had willingly participated as Secretary of State in the Washington administration after expressing time and again his general approval of the new Constitution. But it was not long before he became disenchanted with the direction the new government was taking under the leadership of Alexander Hamilton, the dominant figure in those early years. Jefferson provided the philosophical basis for making American government more democratic. He defined a republic as "a government by its citizens in mass, acting directly and personally, according to rules established by the majority." For him a republic was a form of government in which action was taken "by the citizens in person, in affairs within their reach and competence; in all others by representatives chosen immediately, and removable by themselves." For Jefferson then, at least theoretically, "republic" and "democracy" were synonymous. When he became our third President, he summed up his views in a thoughtful inaugural address. First, in regard to republican government as he defined it, he said:

I know, indeed, that some honest men fear that a republican government can not be strong, that this Government is not strong enough; but would the honest patriot, in the full tide of successful experiment, abandon a government which has so far kept us free and firm, on the theoretic and visionary fear that this Government, the world's best hope, may by possibility want energy to preserve itself? I trust not. I believe this, on the contrary, the strongest Government on earth. I believe it is the only one where every man, at the call of the law, would fly to the standard of the law, and would meet invasions of the public order as his own personal concern. Sometimes it is said that man cannot be trusted with the government of himself. Can he, then, be trusted with the government of others? Or have we found angels in the forms of kings to govern him? Let history answer this question.

For Jefferson, then, since there were no angels to act as kings, the only alternative was majority rule. In his inaugural address he made it crystal clear that he believed in majority rule: "About to enter, fellow-citizens, on the exercise of duties which comprehend everything dear and valuable to you, it is proper you should understand what I deem the essential principles of our Government . . . ; a jealous care of the right of election by the people—a mild and safe corrective of abuses which are lopped by the sword of revolution where peaceable remedies are unprovided; *absolute acquiescence in the decisions of the majority,* the vital principle of republics, from which is no appeal but to force, the vital principle and immediate parent of despotism . . ." (italics supplied).

Jefferson's devotion to majority rule did not mean that he had little regard for individual rights. One need only recall his magnificent words in the Declaration of Independence to appreciate Jefferson's devotion to individual rights. He reiterated these thoughts in his inaugural address: "All, too, will bear in mind this sacred principle, that though the will of the majority is in all cases to prevail, that will, to be rightful, must be reasonable; that the minority possess their equal rights, which equal law must protect, and to violate which would be oppression." Unlike the Founding Fathers, for Jefferson, there was no dichotomy between majority rule and individual rights. For him, majority rule was the best, not the perfect, way to protect individual rights. ". . . we may say with truth and meaning, that governments are more or less republican, as they have more or less of the element of popular election and control in their composition: and believing, as I do, that the mass of the citizens is the safest depository of their own rights, and especially, that the evils flowing from the duperies of the people, are less injurious than those from the egoism of their agents, I am a friend to that composition of government which has in it the most of this ingredient." Again, he wrote to a friend in 1816: "Do not be frightened . . . by the alarms of the timid, or the croakings of wealth against the ascendency of the people. If experience be called for, appeal to that of our fifteen or twenty governments for forty years, and show me where the people have done half the mischief in these forty years, that a single despot would have done in a single year; or show half the riots and rebellions, the crimes and the punishments, which have taken place in any single nation, under kingly government, during the same period."

Jefferson's words and ideas made an impact on the thoughts and actions of many who came after him. In short order, partly as a consequence of his ideas, property qualifications for voters were dropped in most states, and the franchise was extended to more people. More and more governmental officials were elected by popular vote instead of being appointed by legislatures. Voters participate more directly in the election of the President than they did in the early days. Senators are now elected directly by the voters of their respective states rather than by the state legislators. On the state level, the instrumentalities of initiative, referendum, and recall have been established, and in some states even judges are now elected.

One of the consequences of the inexorable drive toward more democratic government was the enhancement of the word "democracy" itself. This is probably due as much to the literati like Emerson, Thoreau, and Whitman as to political leaders like Jackson and Wilson. As the connotation of the word became more and more favorable, it was only natural that political protagonists for one cause or another would attempt to invoke it. As long as the word had the precise meaning of government by the people, it was impossible for advocates of nondemocratic institutions and policies to urge that what they were advocating was democracy. Consequently, they attempted to redefine democracy as being the republican form of government the Founding Fathers set up, or the sum total of American institutions and practice up to the point of controversy. A good example of the attempt to redefine "democracy" came at the time President Franklin D. Roosevelt attempted to change the composition of the Supreme Court in 1937. The Senate Judiciary Committee in its adverse report on the Roosevelt plan had this to say:

> We are told that a reactionary oligarchy defies the will of the majority, that this is a bill to "unpack" the Court and give effect to the desires of the majority; that is to say, a bill to increase the number of Justices for the express purpose of neutralizing the views of some of the present members. . . . This amounts to nothing more than the declaration that when the Court stands in the way of a legislative enactment, the Congress may reverse the ruling by enlarging the Court. When such a principle is adopted, our constitutional system is overthrown! . . .
>
> Even if every charge brought against the so-called "reactionary" members of this Court be true, it is far better that we await orderly but inevitable change of personnel than that we impatiently overwhelm them with new members. Exhibiting this restraint, thus demonstrating our faith in the American system, we shall set an example that will protect the independent American judiciary from attack as long as this Government stands.

Summing up, the Committee asserted that "It [the proposal] stands now before the country, acknowledged by its proponents as a plan to force judicial interpretation of the Constitution, a proposal that *violates every sacred tradition of American democracy*" (italics supplied).

As a consequence of such use of the word "democracy" in our debates over public policy, the meaning of the word has become fuzzy. It is used variously to describe the sum of all our present institutions and practices, what the Framers intended and a whole host of other things. During World War II some commentators went so far afield as to equate democracy with eating hot dogs at Yankee Stadium while watching the Yankees play baseball.

The real significance of the confusion over the meaning of "democracy" is that it reflects an ambivalence about majority rule. There is no unanimity of opinion in the United States regarding the desirability of unfettered majority rule. Although many of us give lip service to the concept of majority rule, at the same time many of us like the checks and balances of our present system. How many are prepared to do away with judicial review, for instance? We are as a people, however, fairly single-minded about the *purpose* of government. The vast majority of Americans regard the *purpose* of government as the *enhancement of the value and dignity of the*

uncertainty

individual. This concept, of course, comprehends the three universal purposes of government discussed earlier, and places special emphasis on the third of these, the development of the individual. But from the beginning, there has been lively debate in our country over how to achieve this purpose. It is obvious from our institutions that we as a people are not prepared, at least yet, to submit completely to majority rule. As indicated earlier, we have, however, over the years removed some of the fetters placed on majority rule by the Framers of the Constitution.

As pointed out earlier, the difficulty inherent in characterizing governments as either democratic or authoritarian is that the terms will not precisely define all the governments which rest in each category. Employing such a dichotomy means that the rough measure for categorizing governments as one or the other must be the extent of popular participation in the government. Those political systems which allow for a great deal of it in the form of free elections and the exercise of great and real political power by elected representatives are democracies. Obviously, some systems allow for more popular participation than others and it would seem a fair statement that those that do are more democratic. For example, wouldn't it be accurate and meaningful to state that the government of Great Britain is more democratic than the government of the United States? In England, the House of Commons, the popularly elected legislature, makes the law of the land. Although England has an unwritten Constitution, Commons is free to pass whatever legislation it deems to be constitutional. Nor can that legislation be vetoed by the Chief Executive or declared unconstitutional by the courts. Both the Prime Minister, the Chief Executive, and the Cabinet, the chief executive officers, are selected by the legislature, although nominally appointed by the Monarch. If the Prime Minister and his Cabinet lose the "confidence" of Commons, they resign. Usually new elections are held when a Prime Minister and Cabinet fall. Patently, rule by the majority in Britain is more direct and unfettered than in the United States. This does not mean, of course, that the British government is better or worse. We are not trying to settle the question of what degree of democracy is more desirable. That is a question which you must answer for yourself. Our only point in comparing the basic points of the English government against our own at this time is to indicate that there are differences between governments categorized as democracies. Also, it is clear that it is fair to say that one government is more democratic than another without placing a value judgment on such a conclusion.

To digress for a moment, one question which has perennially fascinated students of government is "How do you classify an authoritarian government which has been installed in power by vote of the majority?" And this is not an academic question; it has happened. Professor Herbert McCloskey has argued persuasively that the majority in a democracy has neither the moral nor legal right to vote themselves out of power.[1] But for our purposes of classification, if a majority does relinquish permanently the power to govern to a few, they have changed their form of government effectively from a democratic one to an authoritarian one.

THE ARGUMENT FOR
UNFETTERED DEMOCRACY

The case for government by the people through their elected representatives without checks and balances is based on four major propositions. The first proposition is that government is the agent of the people, that its only justification is as a means to achieve the aspirations of the people of the society. The second proposition is that all people are inherently equal. This is not to say that all people are of equal talents but rather that each of us has equal worth in the eyes of God, an equal right to live and to seek fulfillment in life. As John Locke put it: "Man being born, as has been proved, with a title to perfect freedom and uncontrolled enjoyment of all rights and privileges of the law of nature, equally with any other man, or number of men in the world." There has been a lively argument throughout American history as to what Thomas Jefferson meant when he wrote in the Declaration of Independence that "We hold these truths to be self-evident, that all men are created equal, that they are endowed by their Creator with certain unalienable rights, that among these are Life, Liberty and the Pursuit of Happiness." In face of the argument that all men are not equal in talent and ability, Abraham Lincoln replied:

I think the authors of that notable instrument intended to include *all* men, but they did not intend to declare all men equal in *all* respects.

[1] Herbert McCloskey, "The Fallacy of Absolute Majority Rule," 11 *Journal of Politics*, 637 (1949).

They did not mean to say all were equal in color, size, intellect, moral developments, or social capacity. They defined with tolerable distinctness in what respects they did consider all men created equal—equal with "certain inalienable rights, among which are life, liberty, and the pursuit of happiness." This they said, and this they meant. They did not mean to assert the obvious untruth that all were then actually enjoying that equality nor yet that they were about to confer it immediately upon them. In fact, they had no power to confer such a boon. They meant simply to declare the right, so that enforcement of it might follow as fast as circumstances should permit.

To the proposition that all men are inherently equal, it is a corollary that the government set up to serve all must serve each equally. These two propositions support and are supported by the "contract theory" of government, the theory that government is a *contract* in two senses: among the people to institute a government, and between the people and their government. The theory is predicated on three premises: (1) that everyone, whatever his position, has an equal stake in the society; (2) that government's reason for being is to exercise those powers which the people grant it by the terms of the contract; and (3) that should government violate the terms of the contract, the people have the right to revoke it, by force if necessary.

The third proposition is that the people themselves are the best judges of what is good for them. The idea that some elite or individual can better judge what is good for the people is rejected on theoretical and on pragmatic grounds. The proponent of unfettered democracy asks Jefferson's question: "Have we found angels in the form of kings to govern him [man]?" And answers with Jefferson, "Let history answer this question." Theodore Roosevelt, looking at history, asserted that "The majority of plain people will day in and day out make fewer mistakes in governing themselves than any smaller body of men will make in trying to govern them." To the charge that the individual and minorities will be subject to arbitrary and unjust treatment by the majority, the answer is that it is in the best interests of all that the majority protect minorities. For they must know that there may be a day when they too might be a minority. As Woodrow Wilson put it: "If I thought that the American people were reckless, were ignorant, were vindictive, I might shrink from putting the government in their hands. But the beauty of democracy is that when you are reckless you destroy your own established conditions of life; when you are vindictive, you wreak vengeance upon yourself; the whole stability of a democratic policy rests upon the fact that every interest is every man's interest." In actual fact, we know that majorities can be cavalier with the rights of minorities. Yet proponents of unfettered democracies believe that in the *long run* minorities will be better protected in a truly democratic society than in any other. This brings us to proposition four: majority rule is better than any other form of government. It is not fair to match majority rule against some perfect system because no such perfect system exists. We must compare it with the alternatives. Protagonists for more democracy would argue that every system short of unfettered majority rule is worse. They agree with Winston Churchill's witty dictum that "Democracy is the worst form of government except for all others that have been tried."

THE ARGUMENT FOR
A MODIFIED DEMOCRACY

Traditionally, those who argue the case for a modified democracy generally accept propositions one and two, as well as four, provided that it is the kind of democracy they advocate, rather than unfettered democracy, that is being compared with other forms of government. Where they part company with proponents of unfettered democracy is on proposition three. Many, like the Founding Fathers, fear that an unbridled majority will do violence to the rights of individuals and minorities. They agree with the view which, as we saw earlier, was so forcibly expressed by Madison, that unfettered democracies "have ever been spectacles of turbulence and contention; have ever been found incompatible with personal security or the rights of property; and have in general been as short in their lives as they have been violent in their deaths."

To those who would point to the British experience and draw from it the inference that where the unfettered majority rules it is possible to have a high regard for individual liberties—for, in truth, the British have an exceptionally fine record in the protection of individual civil liberties—the answer is made that it would not be true everywhere. The modifiers point to the numerous instances in the American experience when a President's veto or the Senate's temperance has prevented precipitous action on the part of the

people's representatives on the national level, and when judicial review exercised by the Supreme Court served to constrain unconstitutional actions of state legislatures. Consequently, these people urge
the retention of the checks on majority rule which the Founding
Fathers set forth in the Constitution.

However meticulous a majority may be of minority rights, unfettered majority rule is unacceptable to some modifiers on still another basis. There are those among them who argue that questions
of public policy are so complex in the modern state that the average
man cannot possibly understand the issues. Since the solution of
some of these issues is a life and death matter, it is not only foolish
but dangerous to rely upon the general public to solve problems like
determining whether H-Bomb tests should be continued. Instead,
they suggest that the public should happily relinquish the reins
of government to a few elected officials, subjecting them to scrutiny
and an occasional vote of confidence or recall. The best statement
of this position is Walter Lippmann's *Public Philosophy*.[2] Although
we will analyze his thesis and quote from it extensively, all students
of government should read it in its entirety, for it constitutes a chal-
lenging attack on traditional democratic theory. Lippmann states:

. . . there has developed in this century a functional derangement of
the relationship between the mass of the people and the government. The
people have acquired power which they are incapable of exercising, and
the governments they elect have lost powers which they must recover if
they are to govern. What then are the true boundaries of the people's
power? The answer cannot be simple. But for a rough beginning let us
say that the people are able to give and to withhold their consent to
being governed—their consent to what the government asks of them,
proposes to them, and has done in the conduct of their affairs. They can
elect the government. They can remove it. They can approve or disapprove its performance. But they cannot administer the government.
They cannot themselves perform. They cannot normally initiate and
propose the necessary legislation. A mass cannot govern. The people, as
Jefferson said, are not "qualified to exercise themselves the Executive
Department; but they are qualified to name the person who shall exercise it. . . . They are not qualified to legislate; with us therefore they
only choose the legislators."

Where mass opinion dominates the government, there is a morbid
derangement of the true functions of power. The derangement brings

about the enfeeblement, verging on paralysis, of the capacity to govern. This breakdown in the constitutional order is the cause of the precipitate and catastrophic decline of Western society. It may, if it cannot be arrested and reversed, bring about the fall of the West.

Nor does Lippmann see any hope in the possibility of ever achieving an educated and enlightened public opinion on specific crucial issues.

The unhappy truth is that the prevailing public opinion has been destructively wrong at the critical junctures. The people have imposed a veto upon the judgments of informed and responsible officials. They have compelled the governments, which usually knew what would have been wiser, or was necessary, or was more expedient, to be too late with too little, or too long with too much, too pacifist in peace and too bellicose in war, too neutralist or appeasing in negotiation or too intransigent. Mass opinion has acquired mounting power in this century. It has shown itself to be a dangerous master of decisions when the stakes are life and death. . . .

The errors of public opinion in these matters have a common characteristic. The movement of opinion is slower than the movement of events. Because of that, the cycle of subjective sentiments on war and peace is usually out of gear with the cycle of objective developments. Just because they are mass opinions there is an inertia in them. It takes much longer to change many minds than to change a few. It takes time to inform and to persuade and to arouse large scattered varied multitudes of persons. So before the multitude have caught up with the old events there are likely to be new ones coming up over the horizon with which the government should be preparing to deal. But the majority will be more aware of what they have just caught up with near at hand than with what is still distant and in the near future. For these reasons the propensity to say No to a change of course sets up a compulsion to make mistakes. The opinion deals with a situation which no longer exists.

As Lippmann sees it, government officers dependent upon capricious voters for their positions cannot be effective leaders.

In government offices which are sensitive to the vehemence and passion of mass sentiment public men have no sure tenure. They are in effect perpetual office seekers, always on trial for their political lives, always required to court their restless constituents. They are deprived of their independence. Democratic politicians rarely feel they can afford the luxury of telling the whole truth to the people. And since not telling it, though prudent, is uncomfortable, they find it easier if they themselves do not have to hear too often too much of the sour truth. The men under them who report and collect the news come to realize in their turn that it is safer to be wrong before it has become fashionable to be right.

With exceptions so rare that they are regarded as miracles and freaks of nature, successful democratic politicians are insecure and intimidated men. They advance politically only as they placate, appease, bribe, seduce, bamboozle, or otherwise manage to manipulate the demanding and threatening elements in their constituencies. The decisive consideration is not whether the proposition is good but whether it is popular—not whether it will work well and prove itself but whether the active talking constituents like it immediately. Politicians rationalize this servitude by saying that in a democracy public men are the servants of the people.

This devitalization of the governing power is the malady of democratic states. As the malady grows the executives become highly susceptible to encroachment and usurpation by elected assemblies; they are pressed and harassed by the higgling of parties, by the agents of organized interests, and by the spokesmen of sectarians and ideologues. The malady can be fatal. It can be deadly to the very survival of the state as a free society if, when the great and hard issues of war and peace, of security and solvency, of revolution and order are up for decision, the executive and judicial departments, with their civil servants and technicians, have lost their power to decide.

At no point, however, does Lippmann suggest that the people should have no voice in their government.

The executive is the active power in the state, the asking and the proposing power. The representative assembly is the consenting power, the petitioning, the approving and the criticizing power, the accepting and refusing power. The two powers are necessary if there is to be order and freedom. But each must be true to its own nature, each limiting and complementing the other. The government must be able to govern and the citizens must be represented in order that they shall not be oppressed. The health of the system depends upon the relationship of the two powers. If either absorbs or destroys the functions of the other power, the constitution is deranged.

Lippmann suggests that the only way out is for the voters to recognize their limitations and for the elected officials to understand their real mission.

The implied principle may be defined in other terms by saying that while the electors choose the ruler, they do not own any shares in him and they have no right to command him. His duty is to the office and not to his electors. Their duty is to fill the office and not to direct the officeholder. I realize that, as I have stated it, the principle runs counter to the popular view that in a democracy public men are the servants (that is, the agents) of the people (that is, of the voters).

Note carefully, however, that Lippmann is not advocating doing away with popular participation in government. What he is advocating is that the people exercise more self-restraint and allow the elected leaders to rule.

In rejoinder, proponents of unfettered democracy would say that they do not take issue with Lippmann's contention that the vast army of people who constitute the majority of a large nation should refrain from trying to perform the functions of the executive branch of the government. They would urge only that the electorate should perform the legislative function as described by Lippmann. They would argue that what Lippmann describes as the "devitalization of the governing power" has in truth been a devitalization of leadership. They would say that it is, perhaps, true that political leaders in democratic societies in recent decades have toadied to what they conceive to be public opinion but this only manifests a lack of faith in the people by their leaders. They would assert that leaders are too prone to sell the people short and to assume that they will not understand the issues, this sometimes in the face of impressive evidence to the contrary. For example, before World War II, it was clearly demonstrated by frequent polls in the United States that a majority of the people favored some kind of universal military training. Yet the leaders, operating on the assumption that the people would not really be for what the leadership considered a necessity, never gave the people a chance to vote on the issue; the men most prominent in both parties refrained from pressing for universal military training. The devotees of unfettered democracy would say that there is nothing in democratic theory which precludes vital and dynamic leadership. As a matter of fact, democracy like any other human institution works best when there is first-rate leadership. They would assert that, when the people are confronted properly with the issues by straight-talking leaders, they will approve wise policies most of the time and disapprove the unwise ones. And that no small group of elite will be right more often than the majority. Finally, they would argue that, if the people can be depended upon to determine which leaders will be good ones (an implicit assumption of Lippmann's), they can only do so on terms of how these leaders handle specific situations and for what policies they stand.

THE RATIONALE FOR
AUTHORITARIAN GOVERNMENT

As might well be expected, authoritarians challenge all of the basic assumptions on which the case for democracy is based. The rationale for authoritarianism is premised on the converse of these assumptions. Whereas the democrat sees government as the servant of the people, the authoritarian reverses the order of things. As one of the spokesmen for Italian fascism, Alfredo Rocco, put it:

The relations therefore between state and citizens are completely reversed by the Fascist doctrine. Instead of the liberal-democratic formula, "society for the individual" we have, "individuals for society" with this difference however: that while the liberal doctrines eliminated society, Fascism does not submerge the individual in the social group. It subordinates him, but does not eliminate him; the individual as a part of his generation ever remaining an element of society however transient and insignificant he may be. Moreover the development of individuals in each generation, when coordinated and harmonized, conditions the development and prosperity of the entire social unit.

At this juncture the antithesis between the two theories must appear complete and absolute. Liberalism, Democracy, and Socialism look upon social groups as aggregates of living individuals; for Fascism they are the recapitulating unity of the indefinite series of generations. For Liberalism, society has no purposes other than those of the members living at a given moment. For Fascism, society has historical and immanent ends of preservation, expansion, improvement, quite distinct from those of the individuals which at a given moment compose it; so distinct in fact that they may even be in opposition. Hence the necessity, for which the older doctrines make little allowance, of sacrifice, even up to the total immolation of individuals, in behalf of society; hence the true explanation of war, eternal law of mankind, interpreted by the liberal-democratic doctrines as a degenerate absurdity or as a maddened monstrosity.[3]

Rocco goes on to sum up the general view of the authoritarians: "For Liberalism, the individual is the end and society the means;

---

[3] Alfredo Rocco, *The Political Doctrine of Fascism* (Worcester: Carnegie Endowment for International Peace, 1926), p. 18.

nor is it conceivable that the individual, considered in the dignity of an ultimate finality, be lowered to mere instrumentality. For Fascism [substitute any authoritarianism], society is the end, individuals the means, and its whole life consists in using individuals as instruments for social ends." [4]

The rationale for making society rather than the individual the end is that society has a "continuous life over and beyond the existence of the several individuals." Thus Hitler used to refer to the "Greater Reich," a great future German state, as the ultimate goal for the German people toward which all their efforts must be directed. In the same fashion, communist leaders today regard a communist world as the ultimate goal to which all individuals under their dominion should be willing to sublimate all their interests.

In this connection, it is worth reflecting on the startling words of Rocco regarding war which have been quoted above. What he is saying in effect is that in democracies war must always be regarded as a "degenerate absurdity" or a "maddened monstrosity." And it is quite true that if you regard the individual as all-important, war which endangers the lives of individuals is repugnant to you. As a matter of fact, in modern times democratic governments have engaged in warfare only when they felt that it was essentially a matter of self-preservation. The British, French, and Americans became involved in the great wars of this century only when they felt convinced their own survival depended upon it. In contrast, Hitler frequently asserted that the attaining of the "Greater Reich" was worth millions of present German lives. In view of the difference in theory as regards the individual and society, it is not surprising that authoritarian governments have been much more prone to start wars than democratic governments. It would be much more difficult, for example, to convince the American people to precipitate a war than it would be for the leaders of an authoritarian government to decide that the long-range good of the state requires the sacrifice of so many of their minions. This is not to imply that authoritarians will war for the sake of warring but rather that they will be less reluctant to use war as a means of achieving what they regard as the ultimate ends of their governments.

The authoritarian rejects the idea that men are inherently equal. As was pointed out earlier, the democrat makes this assumption on the basis of his ideas about God and the universe. It is not surprising

---

[4] *Ibid.*, p. 19.

then, that authoritarians like the fascist, nazi, and communist who regard God and religion as a hoax find the assumption false. They look at the world about them and observe that men are never equal politically.

As Mussolini saw it, "Fascism denies, in democracy, the absurd conventional untruth of political equality dressed out in the garb of collective irresponsibility, and myth of 'happiness' and indefinite progress." Likewise, Lenin saw that as a reality of life political equality is never achieved, at least in noncommunistic societies. He argued:

In capitalist society, under the conditions most favourable to its development, we have more or less complete democracy in the democratic republic. But this democracy is always bound by the narrow framework of capitalist exploitation, and consequently always remains, in reality, a democracy for the minority, only for the possessing classes, only for the rich. Freedom in capitalist society always remains just about the same as it was in the ancient Greek republics: freedom for the slaveowners.[5]

Therefore, authoritarians conclude that it is the law of nature for men to be unequal, and that government should be predicated upon this inequality and an effort made to have the "better" people run the government. Hitler summed up this view in these words:

A view of life which, by rejecting the democratic mass idea, endeavors to give this world to the best people, that means to the most superior men, has logically to obey the same aristocratic principle also within this people and has to guarantee leadership and highest influence within the respective people to the best heads. With this it does not build up on the idea of the majority, but on that of the personality.

. . . . .

The best State constitution and State form is that which, with the most natural certainty, brings the best heads of the national community to leading importance and to leading influence.[6]

To the proposition that the people are the best judges of what is good for them the authoritarians give loud dissent. They go much further than Lippmann in condemning the people's judgment. They

---

[5] V. I. Lenin, *Toward the Seizure of Power*, Book II (New York: International Publishers, 1932), pp. 217–18.
[6] Adolph Hitler, *Mein Kampf* (New York: Reynal & Hitchcock, 1940), pp. 661 and 669.

would not even admit that people can make wise choices in elections. Read what Heinrich von Treitschke wrote just before the turn of the century:

> The Presidents of the United States, with a few exceptions, have never been men of great ability, because these are not of the stuff to make head[way] against the flood of slander which envy lets loose over them. There will always be natures of too rare a quality for the common herd to understand; for this reason Goethe will never be as popular an author as Schiller. In the early days of the North American Republic Alexander Hamilton was the most remarkable figure, more so in fact than Washington, yet the populace regarded him as the proverbial dog looked upon the glass of wine. He aroused the same sentiments as William Humboldt did at the Confederate Diet at Frankfurt, for he gave people the uncomfortable feeling that they did not understand him.[7]

Where a small group imposes a government upon a society, it may profess to be doing so for the good of the people even though they do not allow for popular representation in the process of setting up the government, and do not consult the people or allow them the opportunity to ratify what is done supposedly in their behalf. To understand such an approach may be difficult for those who have been brought up to revere democratic ideals. Basically such groups with or without reason feel that they have been endowed with superior qualities and that destiny (or God in some cases) requires that they take the reins. Of course, there are those who feel that leadership in a society is a matter of power and that if they have it they will rule the society and make no effort to justify it. Interestingly enough, however, authoritarians have generally believed, as indicated by their writings, that they have had a duty or calling which compelled them to exercise power over their society.

Adolph Hitler, writing in *Mein Kampf*, was not concerned whether or not his future government would be approved by the people.

> It is more difficult, however, to recognize, in the community of all, those heads that are mentally and ideally most valuable indeed, and to give them that influence which not only is due these superior minds, but which above all is beneficial to the nation. This sieving according to ability and efficiency cannot be carried out mechanically, but it is a work that is done uninterruptedly by the daily struggle for life.

· · · · · ·

[7] Heinrich von Treitschke, *Politics*, Vol. II (London: Constable & Co. 1916), pp. 283–84.

But just as in economic life the able personalities cannot be deter-mined from above, but have to wrestle through for themselves, and ex-actly as here from the smallest shop up to the greatest enterprise, infinite training is given by itself and only life makes the necessary examinations, thus of course the political heads too cannot suddenly be 'discovered.' Geniuses of an extraordinary kind do not admit consideration of the normal mankind.[8]

Lenin, on the other hand, was wont to try to prove that his dictatorship represented the will of the people:

That in the history of revolutionary movements the dictatorship of individuals was very often the expression, the vehicle, the channel of the dictatorship of the revolutionary classes has been shown by the ir-refutable experience of history. Undoubtedly, the dictatorship of individ-uals was compatible with bourgeois democracy. But on this point the bourgeois defamers of the Soviet system, as well as their petty bourgeois henchmen, always display remarkable legerdemain: on the one hand, they declare the Soviet system to be something absurd and anarchistically savage, and they carefully pass in silence all our historical examples and theoretical arguments which prove that the Soviets are a higher form of democracy, and even more, the beginning of the *socialist* form of democ-racy, on the other hand, they demand of us a higher democracy than bourgeois democracy and say: personal dictatorship is absolutely incom-patible with your, Bolshevik (i.e., not bourgeois but *socialist*) Soviet democracy.

These are exceedingly poor arguments. If we are not anarchists, we must admit that the state, *that is, compulsion,* is necessary for the transition from capitalism to Socialism. The form of compulsion is de-termined by the degree of development of the given revolutionary class, and also by special circumstances, such as, for example, the heritage of a long and reactionary war and the forms of resistance put up by the bourgeoisie and petty bourgeoisie. Hence, there is absolutely *no* con-tradiction in principle between Soviet (that is socialist) democracy and the exercise of dictatorial powers by individuals. The difference between proletarian dictatorship and bourgeois dictatorship is that the former strikes at the exploiting minority in the interests of the exploited majority, and that it is exercised—*also through individuals*—not only by the toiling and exploited masses, but also by organizations which are built in such a way as to rouse these masses to the work of history-making.[9]

As to the assumption that democracy is better than other forms of government, authoritarians would agree with that great Ameri-

---

[8] Hitler, *op. cit.*, pp. 661 and 669.
[9] V. I. Lenin, *Selected Works*, Vol. II, Part 1 (Moscow: Foreign Languages Publishing House, 1951), pp. 480–81.

can cynic, H. L. Mencken, that democracy is a ridiculous form of government which exhibits and pampers the individual's depravity instead of enhancing his dignity:

I confess, for my part, that it greatly delights me. I enjoy democracy immensely. It is incomparably idiotic, and hence incomparably amusing. Does it exalt dunderheads, cowards, trimmers, frauds, cads? Then the pain of seeing them go up is balanced and obliterated by the joy of seeing them come down. Is it inordinately wasteful, extravagant, dishonest? Then so is every other form of government: all alike are enemies to laborious and virtuous men. Is rascality at the very heart of it? Well, we have borne that rascality since 1776, and continue to survive. In the long run, it may turn out that rascality is necessary to human government, and even to civilization itself—that civilization, at bottom, is nothing but a colossal swindle. I do not know: I report only that when the suckers are running well the spectacle is infinitely exhilarating. But I am, it may be, a somewhat malicious man: my sympathies, when it comes to suckers, tend to be coy. What I can't make out is how any man can believe in democracy who feels for and with them, and is pained when they are debauched and made a show of. How can any man be a democrat who is sincerely a democrat? [10]

Note in this connection General Franco's views on democracy cited in the article on the following page.

Authoritarians have been deadly serious about the accuracy of their views on the strength of authoritarian governments and on the innate weakness of democracy. In large measure the authoritarians who precipitated the great wars of this century were encouraged to do so by the conviction that the democracies were too weak, too soft, and too degenerate to stop them.

In sum, authoritarian governments are governments in which an elite rules. Such governments range from those which are totalitarian, i.e., where the elite rules tightly over virtually all important aspects of the life of its citizens, to those where an elite rules but permits in varying degrees some popular participation or concedes, possibly, that certain important aspects of life lie beyond the reach of government. The rationale for such a system lies in a belief in the converse of the basic propositions on which a democratic political system is based.

---

[10] H. L. Mencken, *Notes on Democracy* (New York: Alfred A. Knopf, Inc., 1926), pp. 211–12 passim.

Franco Redefines His Spanish Rule

Monarchy Can Return Only by Accepting His Regime as 'Normal,' He Says

By BENJAMIN WELLES

Special to The New York Times

MADRID, Dec. 29—Generalissimo Francisco Franco ruled out tonight any possibility of restoring the monarchy in Spain unless it agreed to absorb and continue the present regime, its men and its policies.

In his annual year-end message, which took nearly an hour to broadcast over the national radio, the 67-year-old Chief of State vigorously denied that his regime was a "dictatorship" or any other form of "provisional" rule. His Government—in power since 1939—is the "normal and legitimate" one for Spain, he asserted.

General Franco made no reference to Don Juan, the 44-year-old Count of Barcelona and pretender to the throne, nor to Prince Juan Carlos, 22, who has just finished four years of military studies here under General Franco's watchful eye. But the Chief of State made it fully apparent to the restive monarchists inside and outside Spain that they were still far from easing into power.

"To confuse the continuation of this regime with the proper functioning of a system of succession based either on elections or on heredity is a great mistake," General Franco declared. "The institutions and persons that follow this regime must be in its service. Anything else would lead to fraud."

Thus indirectly brushing aside the monarchists and other political opponents who would like to see him go, General Franco said, as he does annually, that there was a Communist-Masonic threat to Spain and a need for spiritual values that "democracy" seemed to be failing and "order" was imperative.

"Every day the world sees with greater clarity the inefficiency and futility of inorganic, formalistic democracy," the Chief of State asserted.

Democracy, he went on, engenders permanent "cold war" inside a nation, creates the class struggle, provokes periodic clashes between organizations claiming to represent the people and, instead of restraining passions, undermines authority and the social order.

His regime, General Franco said, has created a far better system of representation based on the family, the municipality and the Syndicate (Government-run employer-worker group). This concept has been evolved over the last twenty years, he indicated.

Following his attack on democracy, General Franco cited the recent visit of President Eisenhower, who spent eighteen hours here last week, as honoring the Spanish people and its Government. The turnout of an estimated 1,500,000 Spaniards who cheered the President was a striking example of "Spanish solidarity" behind his regime. General Franco said.

He held out prospects of a richer future to the Spanish people, notably in education, both humanistic and technical.

In conclusion, General Franco paid his customary tribute to Spanish relations with the Latin-American republics, with Portugal and with the Arab nations. He declared Spain would not "obstruct" the integration of Europe based on some "common Christian faith."

ASSAYING THE FORMS

Justice Holmes once observed that "you cannot argue a man into liking a glass of beer." The same may be said of articles of faith which by definition are beliefs which we accept or reject on the basis of deep-rooted intuitions rather than scientific evidence. Even the most learned among us must rely on faith on many of the issues which confront us, because in the present state of our collective knowledge, we have no way of scientifically proving the correctness of the positions we take or disproving the positions which we reject. We believe as a matter of faith either that government should serve people or that people should serve the government. We believe as a matter of faith either that people are inherently of equal worth or we do not. It is impossible to prove scientifically that any of these beliefs is "true." The "facts" used by authoritarians to show that people are not as a practical matter politically equal do not demonstrate that people are inherently unequal in worth. At most, such "facts" may be used as evidence, and perhaps conclusive evidence at that, to show that it is not possible to achieve a society where people are fully equal *politically*. Of course, the democrat would have to concede that it is undoubtedly true that people have never been politically equal in any society, but what is more relevant to him is the idea that where a society does believe in the inherent equality of man and on the basis of that belief seeks, as a goal, to achieve political equality, it comes much closer to it than does a society which rejects the belief and eschews the goal. On this point, human experience supports the democrat.

On its face, it is easy to theorize that governments functioning upon the premises that people *should* be equal politically and that government should serve the people stand a better chance of fulfilling the universal aspirations for government which we discussed earlier than governments which do not. But we cannot stop there, for we know pragmatically that, when it comes to human affairs, practice sometimes makes a mockery of theory. On issues where there is no experience upon which to draw, we must rely on theory. Where there is experience, that experience affords us an opportunity to test our theories. In such situations our theories should serve as hypotheses to be tested in the light of experience. Bearing these

thoughts in mind, the question we should now ask is, does experience support the hypothesis that democratic governments fulfill the
universal aspirations for government better than authoritarian
governments?

All governments zealously endeavor to secure the physical
safety of the people from the elements recognized as criminal in
their respective societies. To some extent, authoritarian governments
with less regard for individual rights and fair process in law enforcement and, consequently, more ruthless in dealing with criminal
elements have been able to afford their people more protection from
the robber, the rapist, the racketeer, and the gangster. But, if history
teaches us any lesson, it is that when it comes to personal safety,
people have far more to fear from governments which they cannot
and do not control than they do from criminal elements. What
threats to safety can come close to matching the ruthless slaughter
of citizens engaged in by the communists and the nazis? Or the slave
labor and concentration camps which they set up? Nor is it valid
to compare the mistreatment of minority groups by democratic
governments with such gross barbarities. Surely, the treatment accorded the American citizens of Japanese ancestry and Japanese
resident aliens by the United States government in World War II,
as well as the treatment accorded the Negro in the United States
for many years, makes it clear that democratic governments are
capable of threatening the personal safety of members of the society
or of permitting some persons to deprive others of their rights.
Nonetheless, there are such enormous differences in the degree of
harshness displayed by the authoritarian governments as compared
with the United States government as to make them differences in
kind. True, the relocation camps established in World War II by the
United States government were shocking in retrospect but they were
not communist or nazi concentration camps by a long shot. Although
some state governments have dealt with the Negro cruelly, their
actions cannot really be compared with the savagery with which
communists and nazis have dealt with large numbers of their respective peoples. Further, it is pertinent to consider that the communists and nazis never have seen fit to admit that the concentration camps, killings, and slave labor camps were wrong. Attesting
to this fact is the testimony of the nazis who have been tried for
their crimes against humanity and the Russian communist state-
ments in 1948 and 1949 on two of the rare occasions when the

Soviets have felt sufficiently sensitive to criticism leveled in the United Nations at their slave labor camps to feel obliged to defend their use of such camps. As indicated by the newspaper accounts that follow, they described the camps as rehabilitation centers and tried to gloss over the harsh conditions which the inmates were forced to endure. On the contrary, the United States government, even while the war was going on, sought to ameliorate the suffering of the Japanese-Americans and after the war sought to make amends by helping them relocate and resettle. The United States government in recent years has played a leading role in endeavoring to secure full and equal rights for the Negro.

Russians Enraged By 'Slave' Charges

Pavlov Assails Mayhew's Talk in U.N. as 'Monstrous,' Likens Briton to Goebbels

By CHARLES E. EGAN
Special to The New York Times

PARIS, Oct. 16—Stung by British accusations yesterday that Russia was maintaining vast slave labor camps in which millions of human beings were treated like animals, Byelorussian and Soviet spokesmen replied hotly in the United Nations General Assembly's Committee on Human Rights today to the allegations.

Alexei Pavlov, Russian delegate, called the charges "monstrous," but his prepared reply contained no statistics as to the number of persons he acknowledged were confined in "corrective" labor camps.

In one of the bitterest attacks yet delivered at a United Nations meeting, Christopher P. Mayhew, British delegate, had called Russia to account yesterday for the existence of slave labor camps and termed a "shameful fraud" the Soviet contention that Russia was a "worker's paradise."

The Russians, who clamored to reply to the accusations yesterday, were prevented from doing so by a Cuban motion to adjourn, that won the committee's approval.

In his speech this morning Mr. Pavlov accused Mr. Mayhew of having used "lying statistics" garnered from Russian "traitors and renegades" in building up the charge that Russia had millions of persons in concentration camps. He added that those in "corrective labor" establishments in the Soviet Union worked eight hours a day, had health and recreational facilities and were paid up to sixty rubles a month for their labor.

Calls Figures Fantastic

It was regrettable, Mr. Pavlov said, that Mr. Mayhew, who called himself a Socialist and Laborite, should repeat almost verbatim the false charges concocted by persons who had fled Russia because they hated the regime there.

Mr. Pavlov said that Mr. Mayhew's charges as to the numbers confined in "corrective labor camps" were "fantastic." He did not, however, give the committee any indication as to the actual numbers held in the work camps.

Mr. Mayhew had said that a conservative estimate would put the number at between 5,000,000 and 6,000,000, although he had heard allegations that at least 15,000,000 were confined in slave labor camps.

Leo Kaminsky, Byelorussian, asserted

that Mr. Mayhew followed the line of Goebbels. In his "hatred and ignorance," Mr. Kaminsky said, Mr. Mayhew had "poured mud" on 200,000,000 Soviet citizens.

"It's a Lie," Delegate Shouts

PARIS, Oct. 16 (AP)—Russia charged today that Mr. Mayhew was a liar and a mouthpiece for fascism in the United Nations.

"He has started a cold war in the United Nations Social Committee," said Alexei Pavlov, Russian delegate.

Mr. Pavlov accused Mr. Mayhew of fleeing the committee today to escape the wrath of the Russian reply. Mr. Mayhew left last night for London. British sources said he would resume his duties Monday at the Foreign Office.

"It's a lie," Mr. Pavlov shouted. "Mayhew's wholesale condemnation of the U.S.S.R. was based on a German periodical written by Goebbels in 1936." Mr. Pavlov said he had looked up the periodical after Mr. Mayhew's remarks.

Mr. Pavlov said the British delegate had reminded him of the story about the man who killed his parents and then appealed to the court for mercy because he was an orphan.

"Mr. Mayhew did the same thing in regard to truth," he said. "He killed it."

"There is a Russian proverb," he said, "that falsehood has legs too short to carry it far."

Another indication as to which form of government imperils the personal safety of its citizens is the procedures it employs in making arrests and holding trials. In this connection, it is relevant to note that, in societies where the people have political power, the law requires procedures which protect them from arbitrary arrests and guarantees them fair trials. Since law in these societies reflects at

Forced Labor Charge Brings Soviet Retort

LONDON, July 29 (AP)—The Moscow radio tonight accused the United States and Britain of talking about forced labor in the Soviet Union "to disguise the fact that slave labor exists in capitalist countries."

The British delegate to the United Nations Economic and Social Council made public in Geneva on July 22 documents he asserted prove that forced labor is an established policy in the U.S.S.R. Britain officially expressed the belief about 10,000,000 Russians were in forced labor camps.

The Economic and Social Council is investigating charges of Russian slave labor under a United States motion of March 7. This motion called for a U.N. commission to investigate conditions inside the U.S.S.R.—a move denounced by Russia as a British and United States plot to get spies into her territory.

Tonight's Moscow broadcast said "the Soviet system corrects criminals, while the capitalist penal system destroys them completely."

The broadcast accused the British Foreign Office of "incredible distortions of the very nature and essence of the Soviet labor reformative policy."

It said the Russian code concerns a strictly limited category of law-breakers doing work intended to reform them and that they are well treated. They work eight hours a day for good pay, the commentator said.

least to some degree the will of the people, it can be inferred that they regard these protections from arbitrary government exceedingly important. Although the record of democracies has not been perfect on this score, the dreaded knock at the door in the dead of night, the holding of persons incommunicado, the third degree, and the summary execution have become the hallmarks of authoritarian governments. Consequently, the people in democratic societies have much less reason to fear that arbitrary governmental action will imperil their personal safety. This becomes even more meaningful, when one considers that in addition to the kinds of crimes against which all governments take police action, authoritarian governments generally view any political opposition on the part of an individual as a crime which requires governmental police action.

It is not hard to surmise why democratic governments have threatened their citizens less than authoritarian governments. Democratic governments depend upon the support of the people. Enlightened people in their more reflective moments understand that if government has the capability of threatening any of the citizenry, it has the capability of threatening all. Consequently, it is in keeping with enlightened self-interest for people in and out of the government to seek to prevent government from threatening the safety of others. Authoritarian governments do not depend upon popular support in the same sense that democratic governments do. They do not have free elections. They depend rather on the suppressive effect of fear, which is best developed by ruthless persecution of those among their citizens who oppose them. Authoritarians, of course, deny that this is the purpose of the harsh treatment of their indigenous opposition. They assert that they must deal severely with "the traitors" who jeopardize the good work being done on behalf of the people. But they so identify their own leadership with what is good for the people that any opposition to them as leaders is regarded as an attack on the state itself. To appreciate what this means, just imagine what it would be like in the United States, if President Kennedy, the Democratic majority in the Congress, and the majority of the Supreme Court justices (who are Democratic appointments) regarded all Republicans as traitors and enemies of the state! One other factor possibly accounts for the way authoritarians treat their opposition. Authoritarian governments have always manifested a deathly fear of any opposition, tending to magnify its strength far beyond all reason and reacting to their fear with the irrationality and intensity common to paranoids. That they will brook no opposition is apparent by their distaste for free elections.

It would be a propaganda tour de force for an authoritarian government to demonstrate to the free world that it had the support of its people. For example, think how it would undercut free world opposition to Castro, if he were to win overwhelming popular support in a free election. But to have free elections means allowing for opposition, free speech, and a critical press. Authoritarians traditionally have been too fearful to allow for such opposition even while proclaiming to the world that they are loved by their people. On the next page there is an interesting account of an "election" in an authoritarian setting.

What does human experience suggest as to which form of government better fulfills the universal aspiration that government mitigate "inconveniences" and encourage the development of the individual? This is difficult to measure. The standard of living is to some extent a measure of a government's contribution to the solution of economic problems. The modern democracies certainly have a marked edge over the societies with authoritarian governments in that respect. But communists argue that this is not a fair measure, for they have had less time than the democracies to raise the standard of living of their peoples. Also, they assert that they are moving faster than the democracies at this time. More will be said on this in the discussion of economics.

The state of the arts and sciences as well as the standard of living is an important indication as to how well particular systems have contributed to the development of the individual. However, judgments as to which nations lead in this respect are arguable. And here, too, the authoritarians can invoke the question of time. They can argue that it is not fair to compare on an absolute basis education in China today, for example, with education in Great Britain, for the communist masters have not had much time in which to develop a great educational system.

To the authors, one measure which seems to be particularly worthy is the degree to which the people of a nation perceive that their aspirations are fulfilled by their governments. And for this, there are good indicators. First, there is the matter of elections, mentioned previously. A democracy assuredly has the approval of

Czechs Ballot for Single Slate
Amid Holiday's Entertainment

Prague's Voters March to Brass Bands and Hear Jazz Concert—Few Exercise Right to a Decision in Secrecy

By PAUL UNDERWOOD

Special to The New York Times

PRAGUE, Czechoslovakia, June 12 —Beside the Gothic arched door of the fourteenth century hall of Charles University stood a low temporary bandstand.

On it a jazz band and two young girl singers were belting out an American tune. About 100 persons stood around listening and watching couples dancing in the street.

When the jazz music stopped, the "oompah, oompah" of a Czech brass band could be heard from the Old Town Square a block down the narrow street.

The scene was the polling place for Prague Districts 25 and 26 for today's elections, in which more than 9,000,000 registered voters cast ballots to fill the 300 seats in the National Assembly, eighty-seven seats in the Slovak National Council and more than 200,000 regional, district and local administrative posts.

One Group's Names on Ballot

There were no contests. The only names on the ballots were those of the candidates selected by the National Front, a grouping of political, union and social organizations controlled by the Communist party—one for each post. The voter's only choice was to accept or reject the candidates presented for his district.

The regime spared no effort to produce a holiday atmosphere. The town was decorated with flags and flowers. Every polling place offered some kind of entertainment—bugle corps of boy

Pioneers wearing red scarfs, choruses made up of blue-shirted members of the Communist youths organization and bands of various kinds.

The polls were in a second-floor room at the university hall. Inside the door were two long tables, one for each of the two election districts. At each sat three officials. At the far end of the room, on a table, stood a gold-painted ballot box decorated with a heraldic lion, the old symbol of Czechoslovakia. To the right was a tall, narrow green screen.

The voters began arriving as the polls opened at 7 A.M. In many cases all the inhabitants of an apartment house marched to the voting center together behind flags and brass bands. At the door of the balloting room an election official checked their registration slips and waved them inside.

Voters Get Ballot Slips

Each voter's name was checked against the registration list and he was handed several slips of paper, each containing one name. A slip represented one of the offices to be filled from the district.

Most voters stepped directly to the box to deposit their ballots, ignoring the screen. However, a woman was persuaded to go behind the screen by a television cameraman making a film of the voting.

Czech officials emphasize that under the law a voter is entitled to mark his ballot behind the screen even if all he can do is scratch off the name on one of the slips to indicate that he disapproves of that particular candidate.

5 of 1,500 Use Screen

Some people have the necessary aplomb to walk behind the screen under the eyes of their neighbors and election officials. One official said five persons out of more than 1,500 who had voted in his district had used the screen.

Individual voters questioned in the election centers as to why they had not gone behind the screen invariably replied that they knew their candidates through pre-election meetings and were satisfied with their competence.

But one voter, questioned outside the center, added:

"What difference does it make? Anybody else approved by the National Front would be just the same."

The general voting atmosphere was quiet and orderly, with a touch of gaiety. The Czechs went to the polls with the air of performing a not unpleasant duty, lingered to enjoy the music and then took the day off.

its citizenry, for its citizens have the political power to reject the system. The very fact that authoritarian governments refuse to hold free elections implies a fear that they do not have the support and approval of the people. Another impressive indicator is the number of people who defect from their respective nations to seek refuge in places under the other form of government. Statistics here are startling. The numbers who have fled authoritarian regimes dwarf the numbers who have gone the other way. Beyond question, these people "have voted against their regimes with their feet." Thousands have fled the authoritarian regime in Cuba. Over 200,000 people fled from East Germany alone before the Wall was erected, largely to stem the flow of escapees. For the communists to swallow their pride and resort to such a crude anachronism as a wall is a good indication of how desperate they had become. Americans were shocked when a handful of American prisoners of war (21 in all) defected to communism. But these numbers were exceedingly small compared to the number of Chinese prisoners who defected— over 14,000.

The authoritarian rejoinder to using the numbers of defectors as a measure of the efficacy of authoritarian government is based on three arguments. First, many of the defectors are enemies of the state and are seeking to escape punishment. Second, many of the defectors are escaping from low standards of living rather than the system itself. Third, the people are not the best judges of what is good for them. The first two arguments can be dismissed summarily. Only a very small percentage of the refugees have been people who had been marked out for punishment before they fled. If, indeed, the refugees are fleeing from economic hardship, that hardship is in large part attributable to the system, as will be demonstrated in our discussion of economics. The real crux of the authoritarian rejoinder is whether or not people are wise enough to know their own self-interest and, in a larger sense, the collective interest of the society. This really gets to the heart of a basic difference in the philosophy of democrats and authoritarians and merits an exploration of the question of whether the people or an elite knows better what is good for the nation. Again, we would like to stress that it would be a gross misrepresentation of the position of those who believe in modified democracy to place them in the same camp as the authoritarians on this question. As indicated earlier, the authoritarian insists that the people are not wise enough to participate very directly or very much in the governmental process. The proponent of modified democracy does not have unlimited faith in the people's judgment but he would be just as unhappy with a scheme which did not provide for important participation. Voting for leaders is, of course, important participation.

Are the people good judges of what is good for them? Let's look at the American experience for an answer.

From time to time, pollsters have pointed up the fact that the American people are not knowledgeable about their government and public policy. There have been polls showing that American voters in large numbers did not recognize the Declaration of Independence or the Bill of Rights, or the name of the Secretary of State. Yet surprisingly, a close study of polls on important issues shows that over a long period of time, the American people have had an uncanny sense as to what was in their best interest. Some years ago, George Gallup spoke to this point in an interview well worth reading in its entirety. Part of it is reproduced here:

"Very interesting," said Mr. Gould. "Because we now have records of the American people's opinions from week to week, it's possible to gauge the value of their views in a new way?"

"Yes," said Doctor Gallup, "it is. We can see whether the Congress or any other group of 'experts' has offered sounder opinions than the people themselves in the past fifteen years. We can point to specific instances and see, in the light of later events, whether the common people were better qualified to govern themselves than any group of wise, or distinguished, or specially trained men who might do it for them. For we have polled them all."

"And have the people been right as often as the experts?"

"They have been as right as the specialists and they have been right earlier," said Doctor Gallup. "This is true even in fields where you might expect expert opinion to be far more reliable than the intuitions of the public.

"Now, take the question of air power. About twelve years ago, in 1935, the military 'experts' were not at all agreed that airplanes would play an important part in the coming war. That seems strange today. Many admirals were then saying planes could never sink ships.

"At that period the people were not only in favor of rearming very fast—which Congress was not, by the way—but they wanted, above all else, to see the country develop a strong air arm. They were more than willing to be taxed to pay for it. And they were right!

"The people did not have their way in this. When we entered the war, we had virtually no planes. But that was the experts' fault. The average man, even in the field of military necessity, had seen things more clearly than the specialists."

"Were the people equally wise in sizing up the world situation as a whole?" asked Mrs. Gould.

"Yes," said Doctor Gallup. "Astonishingly so. The American people saw the danger of a war and they were impressed with the risks of our becoming involved in war without being sufficiently armed. They saw this more clearly than Congress."

"Could this have been a fluke?" asked Mr. Gould. "Or were there other cases?"

"Oh, it was no fluke," said Doctor Gallup. "There are dozens of cases to prove the point the people *do* judge more wisely than Congress —or anyone else."

He tapped the pile of afternoon papers someone had left on a nearby chair.

"Read the editorials in those," he said. "I'm sure that at least one of the things recommended in them today will, in the light of 1950, seem like very bad advice. It's bound to be. No group of men on any newspaper can see the future clearly enough to be right every day. Congressmen can't either. But public opinion, as we poll it this week, won't seem wrongheaded in 1950. I'd bank on that. I've seen it happen over and over again in the past fifteen years."

.   .   .   .   .

"Look at the situation in Asia: as early as 1938 the people of this country were overwhelmingly opposed to our sending scrap iron, oil or gasoline to Japan. Two years later an embargo was placed on these things —but only two years later. It took the government that long to catch up with the people's sentiments.

"In fact, you can take every important step in public policy, from 1935 on, and, with a very few exceptions, find that the people sized up the situation years ahead of the so-called 'leaders' in Washington. Sometimes they are ahead of *any* 'leader.'

"Before *anyone* in government suggested conscription—before the President had even sent up a trial balloon to test its popularity—our poll showed that the people favored the draft. Earlier than that—as soon as the war in Europe started—the general public wished to lift the provisions of the Neutrality Act, so that we could help the Allies. And the people also favored Lend-Lease long before it came."

"Why didn't Congress act on all these things more rapidly, if the people were ready?" asked Mrs. Gould.

"One reason—and a very important one," said Doctor Gallup, "is that in every one of these instances Congress was receiving a shower of letters opposing the very action which the people wanted. Sometimes the letters to Congress were twenty to one *against* a policy which, the polls showed, a majority of the people *favored*. In other words, the people who wrote to congressmen on these matters were not the average men and women; they were an articulate minority. They confused the congressmen." [11]

Dr. Gallup's observation of polling data since the time of this interview has only served to strengthen his convictions. Writing in the *Public Opinion Quarterly* in 1957, he stated:

I have often been accused of believing that "the voice of the people is the voice of God," but the two decades during which I have directed polling of the American public on nearly all the important issues of the day have provided me with ample opportunity to judge the collective views of my fellow citizens.

I am firmly convinced that if, during the last twenty years, public opinion had manifested itself only by letters to congressmen, the lobbying of pressure groups, and the reports of political henchmen—as it did prior to the advent of the sampling polls—the country would almost certainly have been led in the wrong direction at several critical points. The public is almost always ahead of its governmental leaders. This statement has been made many times, and it can be supported by an overwhelming

[11] Gretta Palmer, "How Wise Are We, the People?" 64 *Ladies Home Journal*, 52 (1947).

volume of evidence amassed during these two decades on nearly every conceivable issue—political, social and economic.

Perhaps in an ideal state this should not be the case. But the plain, unadorned fact is that it is true, and anyone who wishes to compare the views of the people, as shown by thousands of cross-section surveys, with official views expressed in Washington, can easily prove it to his own satisfaction. It is my earnest hope that future writers on the subject of polls and pollsters will take time to consult the record before reaching their conclusions.[12]

And another well-known pollster, Lou Harris, has commented:

Voter Intelligence: Some politicians and mass media consistently underestimate the American voter. So-called articulate people have too low a view of the human race, and this talk of an average public mental age of 12 or 14 is nonsense.

Intuition: I've found people far shrewder than they're credited with being. It fascinates me to compare my own impressions of political figures I know very well with the intuitions of men we poll in their homes. I've discovered people can go wrong on issues but they are rarely wrong in assessing what a man is like.[13]

Do not rely on the judgment of Dr. Gallup or Mr. Harris—or on ours. Accept Gallup's challenge and canvass poll data for yourself. The data is readily available. The *Public Opinion Quarterly*, which can be found in most libraries, started once again with the spring issue, 1961, after a hiatus of ten years, to publish the results of public opinion polls. Examine the results of a variety of polls on important issues of public policy and make your own judgment about the wisdom (or lack of it) of the people. Perhaps it would be wise to focus on polls taken a decade or more ago. Hindsight provides an objectivity which is difficult to achieve on current issues. We are confident that after such a canvass you will be favorably impressed with the positions taken by a majority of the respondents.

In part, this wisdom of the voters can be attributed to the fact that most major substantive issues are the subject of long-term debate. The pros and cons are debated extensively in the press and on television and radio. Consequently, when the issues come to a

---

[12] George Gallup, "The Changing Climate for Public Opinion Research," 21 *Public Opinion Quarterly*, 23 (1957), p. 27. He expressed much the same opinion as recently as 1962 in Center for the Study of Democratic Institutions, *Opinion Polls* (1962).

[13] *Life*, May 11, 1962, p. 89.

head, a large part of the electorate is very well-informed. At the same time, many of us have learned a technique of making decisions on important issues by relying on the judgments of leaders whom we've come to respect because we feel that they have tended to reflect our own attitudes and views. George Gallup and Saul F. Rae sum up the efficacy of this form of decision-making in the following way:

By helping the people speak for themselves, the polls have rediscovered the vital truth which the philosopher Aristotle saw so clearly, when he wrote: "A man may not be able to make a poem, but he can tell when a poem pleases him. He may not be able to make a house, but he can tell when the roof leaks. He may not be able to cook, but he can tell whether he likes what is prepared for him." The analysis of public-opinion trends indicates that a man may not be able to decipher a Congressional appropriation bill, but he can tell whether or not he approves of the objects for which it is to be passed; a man may not be able to understand the technological causes of his unemployment, but he knows what it means to be out of work, and his experience will contribute to the solution of the general problem; and a man may not grasp the subtle details of diplomacy, but he can tell whether or not the main principles of his country's foreign policy conform to his standards of judgment.[14]

It would seem then that people are capable of participating wisely in government, but only under certain conditions. The electorate must be relatively well educated and well informed. Consequently, in societies which rely on popular participation in government it is important to extend educational opportunities and to maintain free and vigorous mass communication agencies. Not only is it important to give more and more people an opportunity to get an education but also to ensure that the quality of the education should be such that its products learn the techniques of studying public problems and of making up their minds about them. Specifically, it is important that voters know how to sift sources of information and make reasoned evaluations of the problems posed.

The converse of the foregoing discussion is worth pondering. There was a time when the authors like a good many others felt that democracy was a universal good which could and should be exported to all other peoples. Travel and further reflection have caused us to reassess our position. In backward countries where people

<hr>

[14] George A. Gallup and Saul F. Rae, *The Pulse of Democracy* (New York: Simon and Schuster, Inc., 1940), pp. 287–88.

are illiterate and ignorant about public issues, democracy can hardly be expected to flourish—a fact which authoritarians can be expected to point to as contributing to their case. In short, the *sine qua non* of a democratic society is an enlightened electorate. Nor is there really an accurate objective measure as to how much education and knowledge is essential. But it goes without saying, the more the better.

WEAKNESSES OF DEMOCRACY

To conclude that democracy is a better form of government than authoritarianism for a highly-developed people is not to say that it is without its faults. For it to function at its best, as indicated a moment ago, democracy requires that its people be well educated, well informed on public issues, and highly interested in government. Yet in all democratic societies there is a great deal of public apathy, and the opportunity for education is not always readily available.

A second great weakness of democracy, related in large degree to the first, is the tendency toward oligarchy in all democratic societies. For one thing, the complexities of modern government makes it mandatory that the management of government be turned over to a relatively small number. Further, militant minorities of highly interested people form groups to apply pressure upon the government to achieve the public policies they regard as right ones. As Doctor Gallup pointed out, these pressure groups frequently give a distorted picture of public opinion to the governors. At the same time, because of apathy, most people do not maintain a high level of continuing interest in the problems of government. So it is true that generally the public's affairs are determined by the few and not the many. As a matter of fact, any one who is really interested and ready to devote time to it will find that by working within a political party in the United States, he will come to have considerable influence upon the decisions of his local group, so few are the actual participants. Obviously, this tendency toward oligarchy in practice does violence to democratic theory. Yet ideas for remedying the situation are not easy to come by. Some democratic countries like Australia have attempted to mitigate the problem of lack of interest in government by requiring by law that people vote in elections. But such compulsion raises other problems. Is there any virtue

in compelling a person to vote if he has not been interested enough
to acquaint himself with the issues or if he really does not care which
side prevails? To put it another way, suppose that in a class of 30
students the instructor gives the class the option of taking the final
examination on Monday or Friday depending upon the vote of the
majority. In the first ballot 12 indicate that it is important to them
to have the exam on Monday, 8 say that they strongly prefer to
have it Friday, and 10 say they do not care enough to vote. Suppose
then the instructor insists that everyone vote and on the next ballot
the 10 who really did not care now vote with the 8 for Friday, giving them the majority. Which would be more just or democratic, to
hold the examination on Monday or Friday? True, on the second
ballot the majority of the class chose Friday; yet, of those who
really cared to vote in the first place, the majority chose Monday.

Perhaps it is more of the essence of democracy to base decisions on the wishes of a majority of those who have a real interest
in the outcome. Of course, it is essential to leave the way open in
future elections to allow those who did not vote previously to vote
when they feel they have a real interest. It is not infrequently the
case that some one who feels that it doesn't make any difference
which party is "in" changes his mind on the basis of the performance
of that party in office. Certainly, there seems little virtue in compelling the uninterested and the uninformed to participate in government. This is not to say that efforts should not be made in a democratic society to get people interested and informed. Obviously, they
should be made.

There is a tendency in democratic countries for majorities to
be cavalier with the rights and liberties of individuals. This is particularly true with regard to unpopular minorities or individuals.
Even the many fetters placed upon the majority in the United States
have not prevented abuse of Negroes and religious and political
dissidents by the majority. In fairness, we must appreciate the fact
that the frequent controversies over the rights of minorities involve
situations where the exercise of their rights and liberties involve
conflict with those of others. A Solomon would have difficulty re-
solving some of the dilemmas posed. Should a person be permitted
to exercise free speech by denouncing the religion of others? What
to do about people who want to exercise their freedom of religion
by hiring sound trucks to propagate their faith by noisily intruding
upon the privacy of others? Can free speech, press, and assembly be

used by a minority to advocate a bloody revolution against the majority? Should landlords have their freedom to rent to whomever they please curtailed in order that minority groups will not be discriminated against in housing? Nonetheless, not all abridgments of individual rights and liberties in democracies have been the consequence of such imposing dilemmas. Arbitrary majorities have denied minorities such crucial rights as the right to vote for no other reason than the color of their skins. Doubtless, the record of the democracies as a whole pitted against that of authoritarians on the matter of individual rights has been superior. We must recognize, however, that there is nothing automatic about majorities having a scrupulous regard for minority rights. Perhaps the best answer was offered by the American Framers: to place legal and institutional fetters upon the majority without denying that majority the dominant place in the scheme of government. Or is it too much to hope for that majorities may become so enlightened that they will have a continuous and meticulous regard for individual rights even in time of stress? The British experience would seem to indicate that when a people become politically mature, it is not too much to hope for.

But this is only half of the dilemma. In recent years the peoples of the democracies have learned, in some cases at the cost of national disaster, that democratic governments can place too high a premium on individual rights. In a day when, within the democracies themselves, conspiratorial authoritarian groups are busily at work to subvert the government, to allow such people to do their work unimpeded can be disastrous. The fall of France to the nazis and that of the Czechs to the communists were in large measure attributable to the work of subversives working inside those democracies. So just as democracies may be too cavalier with individual rights they can also be too permissive for their own survival. Democracies must walk a tight line of policy which permits the widest latitude of individual rights and liberties consistent with self-preservation. It is not easy to determine precisely how the line should be walked in specific situations, as is attested to by the difficulties experienced by the U.S. Supreme Court in cases involving the exercise of freedom by those who actually or allegedly sought to overthrow the government.

Even some ardent democrats have argued that democracy with all its virtues is inefficient. Deciding national policy in large legislative assemblies is described as a cumbersome way of doing business which is justified *normally* for what it can't do rather than what it can do, i.e., that legislatures are less apt to be arbitrary than a bureaucratic hierarchy. But it is urged that in times of crisis like a deep depression or war, when national survival depends on effective action, we must discard some of our democratic institutions to save ourselves. Upon reflection, this attitude seems a little surprising in view of the fact that the democracies of the world seem to have been able to solve their practical problems better than authoritarian countries, as reflected in relatively higher standards of living. Nevertheless, one need only to observe legislatures in action to see that there are inefficiencies inherent in representative assemblies. They tend to work slowly, and individual members tend to be parochial in their interests and too responsive to special interests. But, contrary to these generalizations, legislatures have proved themselves capable of speedy and effective decisions in crises. If it can be demonstrated clearly that certain decisions must be made in the public interest, the legislature will act. The issue which usually becomes subject to prolonged debate is the one which is not clear-cut. Where it is essential to have extensive hearings and debate to ferret out all the facts upon which a sound decision should be based, there is no virtue in speed alone in making decisions of national policy.

In World War II, the nazi leadership decided very quickly to go into mass production of a plane which eventually turned out to be inferior to the English Spitfire. This quick but unwise decision eventually cost them the Battle of Britain and possibly the war. On the other hand, decisions about which planes to put into mass production in the United States came only after what seemed agonizingly long controversies in our Congress. Eventually, the decisions made proved to be right. Pertinent to this discussion are the findings of a United States Bureau of the Budget study of the United States at war.

The friends of authoritarian government (i.e., government without a broad base of public participation) have in the past made much of its supposed administrative efficiency in arriving at decisions and in executing them without the hurdles that a democratic system faces in operating through the unregimented processes of public discussion and consent. Such apologists have urged that the exposure of governmental problems to public analysis and decision is a source of delay and weakness and that dictatorship over governmental administration eliminates problems such as this country faced in the planning and coordination of its war effort. These considerations were sufficiently influential in the minds of the leaders of the Nazis and the Japanese expansionists to lead them to the conclusion that democracies could not successfully thwart their designs. It was a fundamental assumption in their plans that the democracies would be so immobilized as to be unable to accept the challenge in a meaningful fashion.

The speed with which the democracies did accept the challenge and the manner in which they overwhelmed those who sought to gain through war suggests that there is need to reexamine the claims to administrative superiority of authoritarian governments.[15]

There is no getting around the fact, however, that President Roosevelt and others of our leaders felt that it was imperative for the executive branch of the government to bypass the Congress in the name of efficiency and the war effort. But this does not prove that the democratic way is less efficient. As a matter of fact, careful analysis of the many executive actions taken by President Roosevelt directly in areas which normally would have called for Congressional action might well show a greater proportion of error than wisdom. In contrast to Roosevelt's approach to Congress in wartime is Prime Minister Churchill's practice of meeting every day with a small legislative group to keep them informed of what he was doing, thus providing them the opportunity to intelligently act for or against him as they might deem wise.

Needless to say, however, France both before and after World War II illustrates how a democracy can be overwhelmed by inherent inefficiencies when it does not constantly strive to overcome them.

DEMOCRACY AND PRAGMATISM

Governments of democracies tend to be pragmatic in their approach to public policy, i.e., rely more heavily on trial and error rather than abstract theory. This stems no doubt from the fact that those who believe in majority rule also generally believe that there are few if any absolute truths when it comes to public policy. One of the few absolutes they do believe in is that the government should operate

---

[15] United States Bureau of the Budget, *The United States at War* (Washington, D.C.: Government Publications Office, 1946), p. 504.

as the majority wants it to. We know from observation that the will of the majority is constantly changing. Critics regard this as a weakness of democracy. They argue that such changing of mind is capricious and foolish. Actually, it would appear that the trial and error approach is one of the great strengths of democratic government. At one point in American history a majority felt that prohibition was good public policy. It turned out to be such bad policy that it was impossible to enforce it. Consequently after trying it for awhile, the majority rejected it. Democracies are more flexible than authoritarian governments. Changes in public policy generally can be made more easily where the measure of desirability is the majority's will rather than some elite's idea of what is right and true. The fault that the majority's will changes means, too, that democracy will be vibrant and alive, for the losers in any public policy controversy know that they can reverse the decisions made against them any time they can convince a majority that they are right. As Reinhold Niebuhr wisely observed, "democracy is a method of finding proximate solutions for insoluble problems." [16] And this is one of its great strengths.

To sum up, analysis of human experience supports Winston Churchill's aphorism, which bears repeating: "Democracy is the worst of all governments except for all others that have been tried." Also, it suggests the wisdom reflected in Reinhold Niebuhr's thoughtful observation that "Man's capacity for justice makes democracy possible; but man's inclination to injustice makes democracy necessary." [17]

SELECTED BIBLIOGRAPHY

The Federalist (There are many editions of this work, at least one of which will be found in most libraries).

GEORGE A. GALLUP and SAUL F. RAE, *The Pulse of Democracy* (New York: Simon and Schuster, Inc., 1940).

ADOLPH HITLER, *Mein Kampf* (There are many editions of this work, at least one of which will be found in most libraries).

V. I. LENIN, *State and Revolution* (There are many editions of this work, at least one of which will be found in most libraries).

[16] Niebuhr, *The Children of Light and the Children of Darkness,* p. 118.
[17] *Ibid.,* p. xi.

WALTER LIPPMANN, *The Public Philosophy* (Boston: Little, Brown & Co., 1955).

BENITO MUSSOLINI, *The Political and Social Doctrine of Fascism* (There are several editions of this work, at least one of which is usually found in most libraries).

REINHOLD NIEBUHR, *The Children of Light and the Children of Darkness* (New York: Charles Scribner's Sons, 1944).

ALFREDO ROCCO, *The Political Doctrine of Fascism* (Worcester: Carnegie Endowment for International Peace, 1926).

HEINRICH VON TREITSCHKE, *Politics* (London: Constable & Co., 1916).

United States Bureau of the Budget, *The United States at War* (Washington, D.C.: Government Publications Office, 1946).

ECONOMIC SYSTEMS

3.

Man may not live by bread alone, but he certainly cannot live without it. Where great numbers of people, living in close proximity, strive to gather their daily bread, there are bound to be conflicts of interest, giving rise to the need for some kind of organization of the economic life of the community. But, even where conflicts do not develop, it becomes apparent sooner or later to all peoples that a systematic division of labor and conventions about the use of some kind of money make for more efficiency and a higher standard of living for the community as a whole. Because of the importance of economics to the life of the community, governments of all kinds become deeply involved in making and policing rules and laws regarding economic activity. So deeply do governments become entwined with the economic life of the community that it becomes difficult to analyze a country's political system separately from its economic system and vice versa. Yet, it is useful for the sake of analysis to analyze political systems and economic systems separately. As in a marriage, where the couple is so close that they come to be identified by the community as a team, the Dolans or the Chases, it is often useful and valid to study the partners as individuals in order to achieve a better understanding of the team.

It is pertinent, too, at this time to point out that too many of us make the false assumption that certain political systems and economic systems must go together. Many Americans believe that democracy and capitalism inevitably walk hand in hand, just as they think that socialism and authoritarianism are inevitably paired. Other pairings are possible. As a matter of fact, other pairings have existed. Some democracies have operated socialistic economies and some authoritarian governments have operated capitalistic systems. But it is probably true that certain economic systems are more compatible with certain governmental systems. Where there is political freedom there is a fertile field for the growth of economic institutions permitting the widest latitude of economic freedom to individuals. By the same token, if government is all-pervasive in the political life of the community there is a strong tendency for government to be pervasive in the economic life, too. But more about this later.

For purposes of analysis, we can treat economic systems under two broad categories just as we did governmental systems. One category includes those systems in which, basically, property is owned by individuals and groups of individuals; the other includes those systems in which property is owned primarily by the state. Of course, as with governments, such broad categories will include a rich diversity of kinds within them. For example, a category composed of systems which permit large-scale private ownership of property will range from the capitalism of the United States to the state capitalism of nazi Germany and fascist Italy. Those systems which embrace the principle of government ownership of property will range in kind from the socialism of England and Sweden to the communism of Russia and Yugoslavia.

THE BASIC ECONOMIC DECISION—
THE OWNERSHIP OF PROPERTY

Since time immemorial every society has had a basic economic decision to make. Each society must decide whether the property in the society will be owned by individuals (or combinations of individuals) or held by the government in behalf of the community as a whole. Many years ago John Locke provided the theory and explanation for the growth of the institution of private property. He wrote that God had originally given the earth to mankind in common. But at the same time God gave man the wisdom to make the best use of it. And according to Locke:

Though the earth and all inferior creatures be common to all men, yet every man has a *property* in his own *person*. This nobody has any right to but himself. The *labour* of his body and the *work* of his hands, we may say, are properly his. Whatsoever, then, he removes out of the state that nature hath provided and left it in, he hath mixed his labour with, and joined to it something of his own, and thereby makes it his property. It being by him removed from the common state nature hath placed it in, it hath by this labour something annexed to it that excludes the common right of other men. For this labour being the unquestionable property of the labourer, no man but he can have a right to what that is once joined to, at least where there is enough, and as good, left in common for others.

He that is nourished by the acorns he picked up under an oak, or the apples he gathered from the trees in the wood, has certainly appropriated them to himself. Nobody can deny but the nourishment is his. I ask, then, when did they begin to be his? when he digested? or when he ate? or when he boiled? or when he brought them home? or when he picked them up? And 'tis plain, if the first gathering made them not his, nothing else could. That labour put a distinction between them and common. That added something to them more than Nature, the common mother of all, had done, and so they became his private right. And will any one say he had no right to those acorns or apples he thus appropriated, because he had not the consent of all mankind to make them his? Was it a robbery thus to assume to himself what belonged to all in common? If such a consent as that was necessary, man had starved, notwithstanding the plenty God had given him. We see in commons, which remain so by compact, that 'tis the taking any part of what is common, and removing it out of the state Nature leaves it in, which begins the property, without which the common is of no use. And the taking of this or that part does not depend on the express consent of all the commoners. Thus, the grass my horse has bit, the turfs my servant has cut, and the ore I have digged in any place, where I have a right to them in common with others, become my property, without the assignation or consent of any body. The labour that was mine, removing them out of that common state they were in, hath fixed my property in them. . . .

It will perhaps be objected to this, that "if gathering the acorns or other fruits of the earth, etc., makes a right to them, then any one may engross as much as he will." To which I answer, Not so. The same law of nature that does by this means give us property, does also bound that property too. *God has given us all things richly.* Is the voice of reason confirmed by inspiration? But how far has he given it us, *to enjoy?* As much as any one can make use of to any advantage of life before it spoils, so much he may by his labour fix a property in. Whatever is beyond this is more than his share, and belongs to others. Nothing was made by God, for man to spoil or destroy. And thus, considering the plenty of natural provisions there was a long time in the world, and the few spenders, and to how small a part of that provision the industry of one man could extend itself and engross it to the prejudice of others, especially keeping within the bonds set by reason of what might serve for his use, there could be then little room for quarrels or contentions about property so established.

But the chief matter of property being now not the fruits of the earth and the beasts that subsist on it, but the earth itself, as that which takes in and carries with it all the rest, I think it is plain that property in that too is acquired as the former. As much land as a man tills, plants, improves, cultivates, and can use the product of, so much is his property.

In short, according to Locke, man acquires the right of ownership by mixing his labor with property. The limitations set by God and Nature on what a man may own are that man must not allow anything to spoil as a consequence of his amassing property. Such a limitation would seem upon its face to prevent the accumulation of property and wealth. But for Locke, the right to accumulate property comes from the consent of men to use money:

But since gold and silver, being little useful to the life of man, in proportion to food, raiment, and carriage, has its value only from the consent of men, whereof labour yet makes in great part the measure, it is plain that the consent of men have agreed to a disproportionate and unequal possession of the earth, I mean out of the bounds of society and compact; for in governments the laws regulate it; they having, by consent, found out and agreed in a way how a man may rightfully and without injury possess more than he himself can make use of by receiving gold and silver, which may continue long in a man's possession without decaying for the overplus, and agreeing those metals should have a value.

The Fifth Amendment of the Constitution bears testimony that the dominant opinion in early America placed man's right to property on the highest plane.

Modern defenders of private ownership of property rely less on the natural rights theory, possibly because such arguments do not make the impact these days that they did years ago. Instead, they point out that pragmatically private ownership has proved itself as the most effective device for maximizing a society's resources in terms of a high standard of living. The United States' high standard of living is cited. As the Hoover Commission Task Force on Business Enterprises put it: "The genius of the private enterprise system is that it generates initiative, ingenuity, inventiveness and unparalled productivity." And they argue that this is no accident but rather a consequence of human nature, that man has an acquisitive instinct and he works most efficiently and happily when he is working for himself. As elder statesman Bernard Baruch told a group of graduating college seniors in 1937:

This is no occasion to compound specific remedies [for failures of our economic system], but I do want to emphasize one general guiding principle which all that I have said before was intended to develop. The means we finally select should *apply* the natural laws that govern us and not try either to repeal or to obstruct them—nor is it possible to make a Procrustean bed of economic theory regardless of human nature and then stretch or crush humanity to fit it.

The moving forces of mankind are acquisitiveness, the urge to function as an individual, a yearning for freedom in mind and body, and above all the constant quest of opportunity to advance. These are the attributes of individualism and the man without them is not worth his salt. We can't repeal human nature by an act of Congress. We can't turn back the tide of world development in science, invention and industrial economy by a cleverly drawn statute.

Obviously, proponents of government ownership look at the matter quite differently. Karl Marx, unlike some of his modern disciples, was willing to admit the great productiveness of the system of private ownership:

The bourgeoisie, during its rule of scarce one hundred years, has created more massive and more colossal productive forces than have all preceding generations together. Subjection of nature's forces to man, machinery, application of chemistry to industry and agriculture, steam-navigation, railways, electric telegraphs, clearing of whole continents for cultivation, canalisation of rivers, whole populations conjured out of the ground —what earlier century had even a presentiment that such productive forces slumbered in the lap of social labour? [1]

Indeed, for Marx one of the inherent weaknesses of such a system was that it would inevitably lead to "overproduction." Marx would hardly have had the temerity of Khrushchev to boast that Russia could out-produce the United States. The sin of private ownership

[1] Karl Marx, *Capital, The Communist Manifesto, and Other Writings*, Max Eastman, ed. (New York: The Modern Library, Inc.), p. 326.

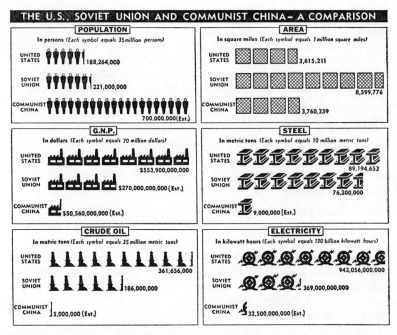

The New York Times, July 14, 1963. © 1963 by The New York Times Company. Reprinted by permission.

for Marx was that it inevitably led to the concentration of owner-ship in the hands of the few and the consequent deprivation of the many. As Marx put it:

You are horrified at our intending to do away with private property. But in your existing society private property is already done away with for nine-tenths of the population; its existence for the few is solely due to its non-existence in the hands of those nine-tenths. You reproach us, there-fore, with intending to do away with a form of property, the necessary condition for whose existence is the non-existence of any property for the immense majority of society.[2]

According to Marx, once property is in the hands of the few, they hire the many to work for them at the lowest wages possible and under unhappy conditions.

Modern industry has converted the little workshop of the patriarchal master into the great factory of the industrial capitalist. Masses of laborers,

[2] *Ibid.,* p. 337.

crowded into factories, are organized like soldiers. As privates of the industrial army they are placed under the command of a perfect hierarchy of officers and sergeants. Not only are they slaves of the bourgeois class, and of the bourgeois state, they are daily and hourly enslaved by the machine, by the overlooker, and, above all, by the individual bourgeois manufacturer himself. The more openly this despotism proclaims gain to be its end and aim, the more petty, the more hateful and the more embittering it is.[3]

Clement Attlee, who as a Labour Party Prime Minister did much to bring a measure of socialism to Britain, attributed the growth of feeling against the institution of private property in Britain to religion. In 1937 he wrote:

Leaving aside Owen and the early pioneers [of socialism], I think that the first place in the influences that built the Socialist movement must be given to religion. England in the nineteenth century was still a nation of Bible readers. To put the Bible into the hands of an Englishman is to do a very dangerous thing. He will find there material which may send him out as a preacher of some religious, social, or economic doctrine. The large number of religious sects in this country, and the various tenets that many of them hold, illustrate this.

The Bible is full of revolutionary teaching, and it is not surprising that, in a country where thought is free, many men and women have drawn from it the support which they needed for their instinctive revolt against the inhuman conditions which Capitalism brings. I think that probably the majority of those who have built up the Socialist movement in this country have been adherents of the Christian religion—and not merely adherents, but enthusiastic members of some religious body. There are probably more texts from the Bible enunciated from Socialist platforms than from those of all other parties.[4]

But like Marx, Attlee alleged that it is the failure of systems of private ownership of property which makes advocates of government ownership:

There is also a realisation that in modern large-scale industry there is but little chance of a man becoming his own master. He is apt to be only a servant of a company. He realises that he might as well serve the community instead of a certain number of profit-takers. The uncertainty of private enterprise which was so manifest during the great depression has made more attractive the prospects of serving the State or the munici-

---

[3] *Ibid.*, p. 328.
[4] Clement Attlee, *The Labour Party in Perspective—And Twelve Years Later* (London: Victor Gollancz, Ltd., 1949), p. 37.

pality. But I think that a more powerful motive which is bringing into the ranks of labour so many individuals from the better-off classes is a realisation of the immoral and unjust basis of Capitalism. The social conscience speaks loudly to-day. Where formerly it impelled people of good will to give to charity, it now leads them to examine into the system which produces injustice. Where formerly they were content to deal with results, they now seek to remove causes.[5]

To Americans born after 1940, who have grown up in a period of unparalleled economic prosperity in the United States, it may be difficult to understand what Attlee was writing about when he spoke of the inevitable oppression of the many in systems of private ownership. There was widespread world disenchantment with the systems of private ownership, as a consequence of the Great Depression of the 'thirties. To understand it, one must realize the tremendous impact that the Depression made on peoples all over the world. In view of the widespread unemployment and hardship, it was no wonder that many came to question the efficacy of the system which produced them. Although Marx wrote long before the Great Depression, he believed such depressions were the inevitable consequence of systems of private ownership. Also, even before the Great Depression, the lot of the many in countries operating systems of private ownership was a far cry from what it is in the present day United States.

We should have learned more, perhaps, from the past decade. Contrary to the prognostications of some communists and socialists, we have learned much in recent years about operating a system of private ownership in such a way as to mitigate the abuses and shortcomings of earlier days. Strangely, critics never took into account such possibility for change within the general framework of the private ownership of property. In this connection, it is interesting to reflect on the experience of Varga, the Russian communist economist who several years back asserted that by continuing to modify itself, capitalism might be able to survive. Since this finding was contrary to the Marxist idea of the inevitability of the doom of capitalism, Varga found himself in deep trouble with the political leaders of the Soviet Union. He later recanted.[6] Nor was Varga the only communist economist to run into such difficulty. See the news account reproduced on the next page concerning a Polish economist.

---

[5] *Ibid.*, p. 194.
[6] Evsey D. Domar, "The Varga Controversy," 40 *American Economic Review*, 132 (1950).

German Reds Score Polish Economist

Special to The New York Times

WARSAW, Oct. 14—East Germany's Communists have opened a harsh political attack against Poland's leading economist and his theory that there might be something worth looking at in bourgeois economics.

The attack was directed against Prof. Oscar Lange, chairman of the Polish Economic Council and a vice chairman of the Council of State. He once was a United States citizen but resumed Polish nationality.

In articles published last spring Professor Lange said the foundation of political economy must be Marxist. But he put forward the idea that bourgeois economy had developed some techniques and scientific theories that might be worthwhile.

In its October issue, Einheit, East German party journal devoted to Marxist theory, charges that Professor Lange's theories are a "slap in the face of all revolutionary workers."

The article said Professor Lange's views were "suspiciously near to views held by certain renegades who for years have been supplying ammunition of the ideological counter-revolution."

Recent experience in communist and socialist countries adds further insights to the controversy over who should own property. The communists have had increasing difficulties in communizing the property of small landholders. Despite the efforts of communist leaders to convince them that it is to their advantage to give up their small farms, they fight furiously to hold on to them. Also, in Britain and other socialist economy countries there has been a slowing up if not a regression in the socializing of the economy. Pragmatically, some hard lessons are being learned. If it is man's nature to be self-seeking as well as cooperative, evidently, a system of private ownership of property will in the long run be better adapted to him than government ownership. Under it he will produce more and be happier.

SYSTEMS OF PRIVATE OWNERSHIP

Capitalism

Of all economic systems, we are, of course, most familiar with our own capitalism. But unfortunately, familiarity does not always breed understanding. If it did, the national divorce rate would be considerably lower than it is. Just as with the term *democracy*, if you were to canvass a group of adult Americans as to the meaning of capitalism, you would get some wild answers. In fairness, it is probably easier to describe capitalism as it was years ago than as it is today. For capitalism like most things in life isn't what it used to be.

In its early days, in eighteenth-century England and nineteenth-century United States, capitalism was characterized by three fundamental features. One was the private ownership of property, with property defined to include land, factories, businesses, and goods. The second feature was that the unlimited accumulation of property was permissible. And the device of the corporation made it possible for groups of individuals to pool resources and build factories and businesses of magnitudes far beyond the capability of all but a very few single individuals to establish. The third feature was the absence of government intervention in the economic realm. Decisions regarding the economy were made by individual entrepreneurs in response to the "law" of supply and demand and competition.

In retrospect it is not surprising that such capitalism led to abuses and that modification was inevitable. Without substantial intervention by government, at least as a "policeman," there was literally anarchy in the economic realm, with all the consequent disadvantages. As a result early capitalism degenerated into a dog-eat-dog proposition. Its proponents in those days did not deny that this was happening; rather they revelled in it. Andrew Carnegie, the great American industrialist, wrote in 1889:

> The price which society pays for the law of competition, like the price it pays for cheap comforts and luxuries, is also great; but the advantages of this law are also greater still, for it is to this law that we owe our wonderful material development, which brings improved conditions in its train. But, whether the law be benign or not, we must say of it, as we say of the change in the conditions of men to which we have referred: It is here; we cannot evade it; no substitutes for it have been found; and while the law may be sometimes hard for the individual, it is best for the race, because it insures the *survival of the fittest* in every department. We accept and welcome, therefore, as conditions to which we must accommodate ourselves, great inequality of environment, the concentration of business, industrial and commercial, in the hands of a few, and the law of competition between these, as being not only beneficial, but essential for the future progress of the race [italics supplied].

Many other leaders in the nation, business, academic, and even religious, held with Andrew Carnegie that the survival of the fittest was as natural in the economic sphere as indeed it was in all life itself. Later the term "social Darwinism" was used to describe this theory because of the elaborate efforts to invoke Darwin's theories about nature to economics.

Almost coincident with its rise, capitalism was modified to some extent by government regulation. Yet in the early days as compared with our times, the economy was relatively free of government direction. Eventually, for the American public, freedom, or anarchy, in the economic sphere with the resulting abuses became intolerable. Before the turn of the twentieth century popular demand forced the national government to make its first strong moves to regulate some major industries, the railroad industry being the first. Also, the Sherman Anti-Trust Act was passed to head off the growth of monopolies and combinations in restraint of trade. Arbitrary action on the part of business and industrial leaders long before the New Deal brought down the wrath of Presidents representing both parties, the Republican Roosevelt and the Democrat Wilson. But the greatest modifications to the system came as a consequence of the Great Depression and the two World Wars during which the government took on a much bigger role in the regulation of economic activities and in addition became much more active as a business entrepreneur itself.

MODERN AMERICAN CAPITALISM / Capitalism has been modi-

fied so extensively since the early days in the United States that it has become customary for economists to refer to the system as a "mixed economy," indicating that it is a mixture of both public and private enterprise. One can hardly quarrel with such a description. At the same time, it is apparent that the American system retains in good measure the three basic elements of capitalism, so that to call it capitalism still has meaning. On the matter of ownership, it is true that the national government is the biggest *single* property owner in the nation. In addition to the public lands, which the government has always owned, the Chamber of Commerce in an interesting pamphlet pointed out that "the national government is making false teeth, operating warehouses, making paint, selling toothpaste, generating electricity, building ships, making rope and is in hundreds of other commercial—and industrial-type activities—competing with similar private businesses." The Chamber further stated:

The government is still the nation's biggest electric producer, the biggest power consumer, the biggest banker, biggest employer, biggest insurance company, biggest landlord, biggest tenant and biggest publisher. . . .

The holdings of the national government's corporations and business-type activities totaled over $55 billion in June, 1954. They had over $1 billion in cash; over $34 billion out in loans; over $3 billion in commodities, supplies and materials; and more than $8 billion worth of land, buildings and equipment.

As explained in the Chamber's publication, government got into business largely as a consequence of war and depression. For example, the government financed and built a synthetic rubber industry after Pearl Harbor "because there was no way for private investors to finance such a venture in view of the uncertainties of postwar rubber markets." Also, for much the same reasons, the government undertook lending and loan-guaranteeing activities during the Depression. What worries the Chamber and others is that once government does go into a business activity, it tends to stay on even after the need has disappeared.

In that connection, by June of 1960, the holdings of the national government's corporations and activities of a business nature rose in value to $79 billion; they had over $5 billion in cash; they had less out in loans (about $29 billion) but had inventories valued at over $20 billion, and over $9 billion worth of land, buildings, and equipment.[7]

Despite these large holdings of the government, the lion's share of property is in private hands, whatever the measure used. A House Committee estimated that in 1948 the government held 27.3% of the total national wealth. Of course, it is disturbing to believers in private enterprise that the government's share seems to grow continually. As the aforementioned House Committee put it:

From 1929 to 1948 public wealth has grown 278.5 percent while private wealth has increased only 78.7 percent. . . . in 1929 the public wealth represented only 15 percent of total national wealth, in 1948 the public wealth amounted to 27.3 percent of the total. . . . The trend continued. Is this "creeping socialism"?

But in his comprehensive study, *The National Wealth of the United States in the Post-War Period*, Raymond W. Goldsmith reported:

No sharp change occurred during the postwar period in the share of government in civilian wealth. Business and households each owned, on the basis of current market valuations, slightly more than two-fifths of reproducible tangible wealth, leaving about one-sixth for the govern-

[7] *Federal Reserve Bulletin*, February, 1961, p. 240.

ment. If military assets are included, the level of the share of government increases, but its relation to total national wealth more broadly defined shows a sharp decline from 30 per cent in 1945 to one-fifth in 1958.[8]

Whatever the trend, we reiterate, however large the government's share of the property, a much greater share still remains in private hands.

No longer is it as easy to accumulate property as it was yesteryear. Where in the period 1895–1913 there was no income tax, the present tax structure is such as to make difficult the accumulation of wealth by individuals. For instance, a childless married man with a taxable income of $200,000, filing a joint return, must pay about 66 per cent of this income, or approximately $135,000, to the national government in income taxes; the childless married man filing a joint return who is fortunate or industrious enough to have a taxable income of $1,000,000 must pay to Uncle Sam about 86 per cent of it, or approximately $860,000. Further, inheritance taxes make it impossible for owners of large fortunes to transmit them to their heirs without the government's taking a large share. But corporations are different. They pay income taxes, to be sure, but not in such proportions as to make accumulations and expansion impossible. Consequently, corporations have accumulated fabulous empires. More than 35 companies have assets of over a billion dollars. The concentration of wealth in the hands of relatively few corporations has been a source of great concern. For the past fifty years many Americans have felt that bigness *per se* in business inevitably led to arbitrary action and restraint of trade. At the same time many of the same people, as well as others, have come to like some of the blessings of bigness, notably research with resulting new products, lower prices, and other significant contributions to a higher standard of living. For example, there is many a man who deplores bigness in principle and buys his car from General Motors and his refrigerator from General Electric, and whose wife shops at the A & P. This ambivalence has led us to do much soul-searching to try to distinguish between bigness which is good and bigness which is bad. We have come to regard bigness as an evil when it restricts competition, but no longer assume that bigness *per se* is an evil.

President Eisenhower in the *Economic Report of the President,* 1957, reflected this view, most accurately:

---

[8] Raymond W. Goldsmith, *The National Wealth of the United States in the Post-War Period* (Princeton: Princeton University Press, 1962), p. 5.

The preservation and strengthening of competition must, therefore, be a leading objective of public policy. It is not the role of Government to regulate the size of business as such, for large as well as small concerns serve socially constructive purposes in a competitive economy. The essential function of Government in this sphere is to foster a competitive environment in which all segments of business can share fairly in opportunities to realize their potentialities. Vigorous enforcement of the antitrust laws is basic to the attainment of this objective, for threats of encroachment on competition are always present and assume constantly changing forms.

Nor does there appear to be much concern that concentration of wealth by large corporations means that a relatively few individuals are holding an inordinate amount of the nation's wealth. Very few of the giant corporations are owned outright by small groups or single families. American Telephone and Telegraph has over 2,000,000 stockholders, General Motors over 1,000,000, Standard Oil of New Jersey over 700,000 and General Electric over 400,000. This is not to suggest that all stockholders hold an equal number of shares. There are still individuals and groups who have very large holdings. But in recent years, even as the corporations have become bigger and wealthier, ownership has become more diffused and the proportion held by the large holders has diminished in favor of that held by the small holders. (It must be remembered, however, that ownership in large corporations is not equated with control. Often the direction of the corporation's activity rests with a decided minority of the stockholders and is largely in the hands of management which may or may not own a large share of the enterprise.)

Despite the fact that it has become much more difficult to accumulate huge wealth, there evidently is still opportunity to do so. The number of multimillionaires in the nation is surprisingly large. *Fortune Magazine* in an interesting article pointed out that there are about 155 Americans with fortunes in excess of 50 million dollars.[9] Nor, as one might expect, is the group made up exclusively of those who inherited wealth. It is still possible for an individual, despite heavy taxes, to accumulate a large fortune. And as was previously pointed out, there are 35 corporations with assets of over $1 billion.

---

[9] "The Fifty-Million-Dollar Man," *Fortune,* November, 1957, p. 176. Also see "Millionaires," *U.S. News & World Report,* January 31, 1958, p. 69, and Alvin Shuster, "Our 398 Millionaires—A New Breed," *The New York Times Magazine,* September 15, 1963, p. 37.

92 Join 'Millionaires' Club'

As Wealth Makes Comeback

United Press International

WASHINGTON, July 15—The nation is producing millionaires at the fastest clip since the get-rich-quick era of the late 1920s.

The Internal Revenue Service—in its latest tabulation—reported today that 398 persons filed returns showing $1 million or more income in 1961.

This was the largest number since 1929 when the stock market was at the peak of its stratospheric binge, and the total of $1 million taxpayers hit a record 513.

92 Join 'Club'

Ninety-two new faces were added to this group in 1961, the biggest increase since 1928 when the number was 221.

The statistics show only those who reported earning $1 million or more during the 1961 tax year. Authorities on the distribution of United States wealth estimate there are a lot more Americans who are worth $1 million today.

Some have placed the number as high as 100,000.

Government tax reports, of course, mention no names. But from these studies, it is possible to get a statistical profile of the average $1 million taxpayer in 1961. It would look something like this:

The average top-bracket taxpayer had an adjusted gross income of about $2 million. He paid about $800,000 in income taxes.

Salaries Small Change

Most likely he was on a payroll, although his income from salaries was a drop in the bucket—to him, anyway. The biggest chunk of his earnings came from profits on the sale of such items as stocks and property.

The IRS Millionaires Club accounted for about .8 percent of all taxes paid in 1961. By contrast, those in the $6000 to $7000 bracket paid 8.4 percent of all taxes collected that year.

Averages are deceptive because the figures are distorted by the few who are high above or way below them. Internal Revenue Service studies on millionaires showed that quite a few ran contrary to the taxpaying fashions of their wealthy brethren.

For instance, in 1961 the reports show that 17 millionaires paid no taxes at all.

Reflects Charity Aid

Their income was canceled out by tax credits, exemptions and deductions. In some cases, this might have reflected big tax-deductible contributions to charitable organizations.

Most of the taxpayers in the $1 million circle owed some money when their auditor figured up the final total. However, five did get refunds.

Nearly everyone in the group claimed deductions averaging out to several hundred thousand dollars apiece—but one member bucked the tide.

Instead of itemizing his return, he took the standard deduction which allows only $1000.

Here are some representative years showing how the trend in $1 million taxpayers has been moving the last 30 years:

1927—290; 1928—511; 1929—513; 1930—150; 1931—77; 1932—20; 1935—41; 1940—52; 1945—71; 1946—94; 1949—120; 1950—219; 1951—171; 1952—148; 1953—145; 1954—201; 1955—267; 1956—272; 1957—223; 1958—244; 1959—280; 1960—306 and 1961—398.

There can certainly be no doubt that the government today takes a much greater part in regulating the economy than it did one hundred years ago. A large segment of the economy is regulated by special government agencies, the Independent Regulatory Commissions. These Commissions have extensive regulatory powers over the transportation, banking, investment, and broadcasting industries as well as labor relations. In addition, the Department of Agriculture regulates a good part of our agricultural activities. Further, government has become the chief planner, though certainly not the only planner, of the economy. By deciding how to spend the vast sums for defense and by undertaking special projects like highway development, it directs much of our economic activity and development. Also, through the setting of rediscount rates and the buying and selling of government bonds on the open market by the Federal Reserve Board and controlling installment buying by requiring down payments, the government can and does expand and contract the money available. Perhaps the most significant development in the government's role in the economy has been the efforts to safeguard individuals from the calamity of unemployment and disability as well as from the insecurities of old age. And the government has undertaken the responsibility for maintaining high employment. President Eisenhower indicated the extent of the government's role in our economic life when he said in 1957:

Government must use all practicable means to promote high levels of production and employment, and to contribute toward achieving an expanding and widely-shared national income, earned in dollars of stable buying power. It must pursue policies that encourage the enterprising spirit of our people and protect incentives to work, to save, and to invest. It must exercise a strict discipline over its expenditures and avoid taking in taxes too much of the incomes of individuals and businesses. It must strive to strengthen competitive markets and to facilitate the adjustments necessary in a dynamic economy.

Our Democratic presidents from Franklin D. Roosevelt on would go at least that far, indicating that the views of Mr. Eisenhower represent a common denominator. Yet, in spite of the magnitude of the government's involvement in our economic life, there is still a broad area of decision-making left to business. Prices of most goods are determined by business, wages above the minimums set by the government are determined by employers alone or by bargaining with labor representatives, and the amount of goods to be produced except in agricultural and oil enterprises is up to non-governmental decision-makers.

In short, there is still a wide area of economic activity free of government regulation, involvement, or planning.

WEAKNESSES AND STRENGTHS OF MODERN CAPITALISM /
Many of the old criticisms leveled at capitalism have grown stale and dated. The American working man is hardly the downtrodden proletarian that capitalism's critics said capitalism would inevitably produce. Taxation, minimum wages, and social security have made for wider distribution of the wealth of the nation. The average worker in the United States enjoys a standard of living much higher than that of the working man in any noncapitalist economy in the world. The predatory practices of the early capitalists have largely disappeared. Much of the credit for this must go to government action aimed at curbing them. But we should not minimize the tremendous part played by enlightened business leaders. Some business leaders have done much to make business more responsible for serving the best interests of the community as a whole out of a new awareness of their responsibility to the community as the managers of the economy. Other business leaders have sought to mitigate some of the harshness of early capitalism because they believe such mitigation is the only alternative to more governmental intervention and action, perhaps, even, to socialism.

Back in 1942 a very highly-regarded economist, Joseph A. Schumpeter of Harvard University wrote a book, *Capitalism, Socialism and Democracy* which attracted a great deal of attention and affected the thinking of many economists. In it, he sounded the death knell of capitalism. He also indicated that his views were not exceptional:

In the second part—Can Capitalism Survive?—I have tried to show that a Socialist form of society will inevitably emerge from an equally inevitable decomposition of capitalist society. Many readers will wonder why I thought so laborious and complex an analysis necessary in order to establish what is *rapidly becoming the general opinion, even among conservatives* [italics supplied].[10]

---

[10] Joseph A. Schumpeter, *Capitalism, Socialism and Democracy* (New York: Harper & Brothers, 1947), 2d ed., p. viii.

Schumpeter's pessimism about the future of capitalism was based on the idea that capitalism was too productive and its environment too static.

The fundamental impulse that sets and keeps the capitalist engine in motion comes from the new consumers' goods, the new methods of production or transportation, the new markets, the new forms of industrial organization that capitalist enterprise creates.[11]

. . . . .

The main reasons for holding that opportunities for private enterprise and investment are vanishing are these: saturation, population, new lands, technological possibilities, and the circumstance that many existing investment opportunities belong to the sphere of public rather than of private investment.[12]

When Schumpeter wrote, the birth rate was declining, and it did appear that there were no new frontiers. Little did any of us dream of the possibility that the birth rate would rise sharply, or that a new atomic and space age would soon burst upon us. Obviously, the basic assumptions of Schumpeter's hypotheses have proved faulty.

Nonetheless, there are criticisms of capitalism which have validity. We still have not licked the problem of unemployment even though we have mitigated some of the disastrous effects by a comprehensive scheme of unemployment insurance. Economies more fully directed by the government seem better able to make work for the total labor force. Also, where individuals are free to enter businesses of their own choice, there is bound to be a large number of business failures. Many entrepreneurs decide to invest in particular businesses on a hit-or-miss basis. Mr. Jones decides he would like to start a new sporting goods store in Wilmington, Delaware. He may or may not canvass the situation very well to determine whether or not there is actually room for another such store to operate successfully in the area. Even if there isn't, if Mr. Jones has the capital to invest and the desire, there is nothing to prevent him from doing so. Or if Mr. Smith, a manufacturer, decides he can produce a woman's purse cheaper and better than those already on the market, and he tries and he can't, he's headed for bankruptcy. In 1962 there were over 15,000 business failures in the United States, nor was 1962 unusual in this respect—figures for the years 1959,

---

[11] *Ibid.*, p. 83. [12] *Ibid.*, p. 113.

1960, and 1961 ran 14,053, 15,445, and 17,075 respectively. Obviously, this is a waste of capital and effort.

In a system which encourages competition and allows freedom of choice of goods to the consumers, there is bound to be a lot of effort expended in advertising, designing, and merchandising which may not increase the standard of living proportionately to the effort expended. For example, if only one model automobile were offered to consumers, with no advertising and no attempt at merchandising, it would be cheaper than current models and presumably more people could own one.

To offset these weaknesses, modern capitalism has some remarkable strengths. First and foremost among these is its accommodation to man's nature. It permits men to seek their own self-interest, at the same time minimizing the risks involved and protecting each from the unscrupulous action of others. The modifications made upon early capitalism have enabled government to police the rules by which men can compete in the economic arena. Also, through unemployment insurance, loan policies, subsidies, minimum wages, price supports, and taking on the responsibility for maintaining high levels of employment, the government has virtually provided that those who lose out in the competition for the high prizes of financial success shall not starve in the streets.

Americans, if not other people, are still interested in leaving the way open to the accumulation of wealth. During World War II, President Roosevelt toyed with the idea of asking for legislation which would limit incomes in the United States to $25,000 per year. A "trial balloon" was set afloat; President Roosevelt quickly determined that such a move would be unpopular. Subsequent public opinion polls proved him right; the vast majority of Americans were opposed to such a measure. In this connection, we have frequently asked our students how many would wish to see such a limit. Invariably the response has been overwhelmingly unfavorable. Surprisingly, when we have further asked, "How many of you expect to earn more than $25,000 per year?," very few have answered in the affirmative. When students are then asked, "Why are you opposed to such a limitation if you do not expect to earn that much yourself?" the answer is a variation on the thought, "Well, I'd rather not foreclose the possibility." Even older Americans who are in situations where it seems a sure thing that they will never have the opportunity

IN ECONOMIC STRENGTH— 1959 FIGURES	IT'S U.S. FIRST	WESTERN EUROPE SECOND	RUSSIA THIRD
POPULATION	179 million	257 million	212 million
TOTAL OUTPUT, OR GROSS NATIONAL PRODUCT	$484 billion	$300 billion	$200 billion
ELECTRIC-POWER OUTPUT	789 million kwh.	450 million kwh.	264 million kwh.
STEEL PRODUCTION *	126 million tons	101 million tons	66 million tons
AUTO PRODUCTION	5.6 million cars	4.1 million cars	125,000 cars
HOME BUILDING	1,350,000 homes	1,900,000 homes	unknown
COAL PRODUCTION	420 million tons	509 million tons	558 million tons
CEMENT	63 million tons	90 million tons	43 million tons
EXPORTS	$17.6 billion	$43 billion	$4.4 billion

Note: Western Europe includes Austria, Belgium, Denmark, France, Germany, Italy, Luxembourg, Netherlands, Norway, Sweden, Switzerland, Portugal, and United Kingdom. Some of the above figures include negligible amounts for other European countries. * Latest 12 months not affected by strike.

SOURCE: United Nations; preliminary estimates by Organization for European Economic Co-operation; U.S. Government agencies. In some instances, part-year data for 1959 were projected for the full year by USN&WR Economic Unit. Reprinted from U.S. News & World Report, March 14, 1960, published at Washington. Copyright 1960, U.S. News & World Report, Inc.

to earn large incomes want the way open, perhaps, more for their children than for themselves.

Pragmatically, American capitalism has produced a standard of living which is the envy of the world. Nor can the high standard of living be attributed to natural resources or to a natural superiority of Americans over other peoples. Russia, China, and India have greater resources and their people have the inherent abilities of Americans, yet they have not been able to achieve the same standard of living. Certainly, the system must have something to do with encouraging such high productivity.

The mixture of private and public enterprise has also proved to be a source of great strength to our economy. Nor should it be

WHAT A WORKER'S WAGES WILL BUY IN RUSSIA AND U.S.

A new Department of Labor study of prices and wages in Russia and the U.S. shows:

TO BUY THESE THINGS—

THIS MUCH WORKING TIME IS REQUIRED BY AN AVERAGE WORKER—

	In Moscow	In New York City
Man's medium-priced wool suit	275 hours	23 hours
Woman's dress	73 hours, 30 minutes	4 hours, 36 minutes
Pair of men's shoes	61 hours	7 hours
Pair of women's shoes	57 hours, 30 minutes	5 hours, 10 minutes
Man's cotton shirt	15 hours	56 minutes
Pair of nylon stockings	8 hours	37 minutes
One pound of butter	184 minutes	20.5 minutes
A dozen eggs	144 minutes	17.4 minutes
One pound of roast beef	82 minutes	21 minutes
A quart of milk	31 minutes	7.5 minutes
A package of cigarettes	27 minutes	7 minutes
Loaf of rye bread	9 minutes	6 minutes
One pound of potatoes	7 minutes	2 minutes

Reprinted from *U.S. News & World Report,* May 9, 1960, published at Washington. Copyright 1960, U.S. News & World Report, Inc.

so surprising, for it is axiomatic that absolute power corrupts. If government runs the economy as a complex of huge government monopolies there is no reason to believe that the government's managers will be less susceptible to the corruptions of inefficiency, dishonesty, and arbitrariness than the managers of monopolies.

When both government and private enterprise operate in the same area, they have a healthy effect on each other. Every power company knows that it is being continually compared to the TVA in efficiency, sometimes unfairly. By the same token, the managers of the government enterprise know that the private utilities are watching them very closely for any signs of corruption. As a consequence of this kind of rivalry, the growth of electric power available to the people of the United States at low rates has been fantastic.

State Capitalism

State capitalism describes an economic system in which property, again in its broadest sense, is for the most part owned by individuals or by groups of individuals but in which the government regulates and controls the economic life of the nation very strictly. At once, you may ask, "How does this differ from the modern American capitalism we have just been reading about?" This is a good question. It is a matter of degree. As we shall see in a moment, the governments of nazi Germany and fascist Italy controlled their economies to a so much greater degree than the United States government normally does as to constitute a difference in kind and justify classifying their economic systems as fundamentally different from ours. Even during wartime, the government of the United States did not go so far in controlling and regulating the economy as the nazi and fascist governments did in peacetime. Of course, as Professor William Ebenstein pointed out, nazi Germany was virtually preparing for war from the moment of Hitler's advent to power and this may account in part for their economic system.[13] Nonetheless, there is no evidence that nazi leaders ever thought that there was a better system to which to revert in peacetime.

In nazi Germany, the government controlled all industrial production by allocating raw materials and the labor supply. There was no free market from which industrial concerns could purchase iron and steel, no pool of free labor from which it could draw on a competitive basis. The Price Commissar set prices for goods. Farmers were told precisely what they could grow, and there were no referendums among farmers to determine their druthers. Nor could a farmer sell or mortgage a family-sized farm; it had to be passed

[13] William Ebenstein, *The Nazi State* (New York: Farrar, Straus & Cudahy, Inc., 1943), p. 234 ff.

on undivided to either the eldest or youngest son. The German worker was literally told in what industry and what geographic area he must work. And work he must, or face heavy penalties. Nor were there free labor unions or trade associations to speak for the workers, business men, or industrialists. All such associations were government-directed and membership was compulsory for all in the appropriate association. These associations were just another means of aiding the government in enacting and enforcing its policies.

The government of fascist Italy was as firmly in control of its economy as the nazis were of theirs. Yet many Americans misinterpreted the fascist economic system of Italy in the 'thirties, believing it to be freer than it actually was, because of its form. The Fascists set up what they called "corporations" in each industry. These were not corporations in our sense of the word. Rather, they were boards comprised in large part of representatives of the employers' association and the employees' association in the industry, associations which were in existence long before the establishment of the corporation. Ostensibly, the corporation had broad powers to fix prices, hours, and wages and settle labor disputes. Consequently, it is not surprising that some Americans saw in fascism an economic system which allowed industry and labor to control and regulate themselves much as our own ill-fated National Recovery Administration was doing at the time. Evidently, they did not read the fine print in the Italian law setting up the corporations, nor did they follow too closely what actually happened under the law. Although the boards were made up in large part by representatives of employer and employee associations, these representatives had to be approved by the "Head of the Government." Also, each board had in addition members who represented the fascist party. All the enactments of these boards were subject to the approval of the "Head of the Government." In practice, Mussolini ran the show. If the boards performed any function beyond being messenger boys for the government, it was simply to give advice. Mussolini made this clear when he wrote:

Fascism desires the State to be a strong and organic body, at the same time reposing upon broad and popular support. The Fascist State has drawn into itself even the economic activities of the nation, and, through the corporative social and educational institutions created by it, its influence reaches every aspect of the national life and includes, framed in their respective organizations, all the political, economic and spiritual forces of the nation.[14]

For Mussolini, then, the corporation was a device for achieving popular support by allowing for participation in the decision-making process without relinquishing the government's power to make the final decisions.

Resort to nazi Germany and fascist Italy as examples of state capitalism should not be interpreted as an indication that the economic system which they embraced is now extinct. They were used because they are the best known and best documented examples. Those who are interested can easily dig deeper in the subject matter and are urged to do so. Professor William Ebenstein has provided two excellent studies for those who wish to pursue the study further, *The Nazi State* and *Fascist Italy*. Spain and Portugal currently operate systems of state capitalism patterned very directly on the Italian corporate system. But more important from our point of view as Americans is the fact that there is a pronounced tendency in the United States in times of crisis, war, and depression, to take on some of the elements of a state-capitalistic system. In wartime America, prices, hours, wages, and allocation of materials have been controlled by the government. In the Depression, government undertook to control agriculture and several other industries regarded as "sick." So, although there is much talk of "creeping Socialism," it is probably more realistic to assume that in any future time of discouragement with our own brand of capitalism, there will be a tendency to move to state capitalism rather than to socialism. Also, there is some logic and allure in the idea that measures which enable us to make the most efficient use of our economic resources in wartime ought to enable us to meet more efficiently our peacetime problems. In short, we have more than strictly academic reasons for scrutinizing carefully the efficacy of such a system.

THE EFFICACY OF STATE CAPITALISM / At first thought, it would appear that to the extent that there was unified overall planning in the economic sphere state capitalism would be more efficient than the modern American capitalism. Still theorizing, we might add, "Of course, this efficiency is purchased at a fearful price

---

[14] Benito Mussolini, *The Political and Social Doctrine of Fascism*, Jane Soames, trans. (London: The Hogarth Press, 1952), p. 24.

in freedom." And most of us prefer freedom to restriction when we have a real choice. But suppose the economic situation in a nation is desperate with large-scale unemployment, depressed agricultural economy, and a multitude of business failures, what then? History amply demonstrates that when people feel that they must choose between freedom and economic distress or restriction of freedom and economic health, they generally choose the latter. Suppose, though, that a people sell their freedom to improve their lot economically and things do not get better economically. It becomes then a classic case of people selling their birthright for a mess of pottage. Yet this is precisely what has happened in nations where people have chosen to switch from freer systems to state capitalism.

In what must go down as one of the greatest hoaxes in history, Mussolini for a time was able to convince the world that fascist Italy was militarily strong and economically healthy. As a matter of fact, by every measure Italy's economy was in poor shape throughout the fascist dictatorship. Even unemployment rose at rates exceeding those of other comparable nations. True, nazi Germany had no unemployment problem because from the moment of its inception, it was on a wartime footing, and we have since learned that even in a freer economy mobilization for warfare tends to resolve the unemployment problem. Certainly, the economies of Spain and Portugal are not so successful as to encourage emulation.

Why is it that unified and integrated control and regulation of the economy, devices which would seem to offer efficiency, do not ensure more efficient operation of the economy? The answer apparently lies in the fact that no one can really comprehend in every important situation how particular plans controlling a huge complex economy will pan out. If the prices of automobiles are lowered in a controlled economy how many will be sold? If the consumers have any choice left, the results will be unpredictable as to exact figures. Yet to control a large complex economy, it is necessary for government administrators to make predictions constantly as to what will happen if particular policies are pursued. The study of economics has not yet reached the stage where such predictions are trustworthy. As one wag put it, "Economists can tell us where we are and where we've been, but they can't yet tell us where we are heading." (Lest you think that the writers, as political scientists, are being unfair to colleagues in the field of economics, we hasten to add that political scientists are in the same boat and the statement above applies to us, too.) As the very fine economist, Paul Samuelson, wrote:

> Because of the complexity of human and social behavior, we cannot hope to attain the precision of a few of the physical sciences. We cannot perform the controlled experiments of the chemist or biologist. Like the astronomer we must be content largely to "observe." But economic events and statistical data observed, are, alas, not so well behaved and orderly as the paths of the heavenly satellites. Fortunately, however, our answers need not be accurate to several decimal places; on the contrary, if only the right general *direction* of cause and effect can be determined, we shall have made a tremendous step forward.[15]

Note that Professor Samuelson uses the *future* perfect tense in the last clause.

As evidence of the difficulty inherent in economic prediction and planning, look what happened when the President's Council of Economic Advisers took it upon themselves to make some very important predictions about our economy. As the late Professor Paul Strayer pointed out to his fellow economists:

> First, the Council has not been content with a summary of conditions and trends in the past but has attempted to predict developments in the immediate future. These forecasts have been well hedged but have, nevertheless, been used by the Council and the President as the basis for legislative recommendations. The results of this attempt at forecasting have been unfortunate. In the January, 1947, report of the President, his conclusion and the conclusion of the Council that there was immediate danger of depression led to the minimization of the immediate problem of inflation. No positive program to check inflation was recommended and emphasis upon the unfavorable outlook for the next year probably weakened public resistance to inflationary policies in both the private and public sectors of the economy.
>
> In the January, 1949, report of the President and the supporting Council statement, the balance was weighted in the direction of inflation. Changing conditions made the President's recommendations for legislative action based upon this prediction seem rather futile almost as soon as they were made. Although the Administration did not push the program in the later months it remained the official program until the middle

---

[15] Paul Samuelson, *Economics* (New York: McGraw-Hill Book Co., Inc., 5th ed., 1961), pp. 8–9. Also see "Economists Count Up Their Shortcomings," *Business Week*, January 5, 1963, p. 18.

of the year. This might have been avoided if the President had not been so firmly committed to the program outlined in January.[16]

Remember, too, in the recession of 1958, the conflicting expert opinions as to what we should do. There was serious questioning of the so-called "tight money" policy adopted by the Eisenhower Administration as a "cure" for the condition of the economy from 1959 to 1960.

In short, there is no magic in governmental control which ensures that government will always come up with the right answers in the economic realm. Furthermore, governmental control usually means the loss of the contribution made by thousands of individual entrepreneurs sweating through the problems and seeking answers. Also, people are kept mentally alert by an essentially competitive economy, whereas under rigid government control the managers and owners of business enterprise become automatons, doing the bidding of their masters. Most of the best thinking on economic problems in the United States comes from nongovernmental sources.

In lieu of having divine guidance, it is helpful to have a multitude of individuals, committees, and organizations seeking answers for hard problems. And again, it is worth stressing that government control always curtails individual freedom.

Socialism

Prime Minister Nehru of India was never more right than when he wrote in answer to the question, "What is socialism?": "It is difficult to give a precise answer, and there are innumerable definitions of it." [17] The difficulty of definition lies primarily in the diverse origins of socialist ideas. Socialism has not been the exclusive property of one national party. It has grown almost simultaneously in a number of different countries. The socialists of each of these countries have given their own particular flavor to the concepts of socialism. Further, in each country the ideas about socialism have been constantly changing. And, at best, at any given time these ideas have been fuzzy because, until recently, socialists have been the "outs" rather than the "ins" in their respective countries. It is one of the political facts of life that "outs" tend to be fuzzier in their ideas and programs

---

[16] Paul Strayer, "The Council of Economic Advisers: Political Economy on Trial," *American Economic Review*, May, 1950, p. 144.

[17] Jawaharlal Nehru, "Nehru on 'the Tragic Paradox of Our Age,'" *New York Times Magazine*, September 7, 1958, pp. 110–11.

than the "ins," who are responsible for putting their ideas and programs into action. Despite the difficulty, it is important that we attempt to reach some common understanding of what socialism is.

SOCIALISM BEFORE 1950 / In canvassing the programs, ideas, and literature of socialists prior to 1950, it is clear that there were three basic elements of socialism as an economic system. First and foremost of the economic ideas common to all socialists was the necessity for government to own the essential means for the production and distribution of goods. The extent of the belief in government ownership and why this belief is held can be measured by these words of Clement Attlee:

> The Labour Party came to power with a well-defined policy worked out over many years. It had been set out very clearly in our Election Manifesto and we were determined to carry it out. Its ultimate objective was the creation of a society based on social justice, and, in our view, this could only be attained by bringing under public ownership and control the main factors in the economic system.
>
> Nationalisation was not an end in itself but an essential element in achieving the ends which we sought. Controls were desirable not for their own sake but because they were necessary in order to gain freedom from the economic power of the owners of capital.[18]

The differences between the socialist and communist approach to government ownership prior to 1950 concerned (a) how extensive it should be; (b) how it should be achieved; and (c) what political system should accomplish it. As we shall see shortly, the communists desired to have virtually *all* property owned by the government; the socialists have been content that government should only own the essential means of production and distribution. The socialists generally urged that government take over these means slowly by evolution, whereas the communists wanted the change to take place abruptly. The socialists foreswore the use of force and in most cases were willing to compensate fairly the owners of enterprises which the government took over; the communists were quite prepared to use force to take over what they regard as stolen property. Finally, socialists desired to maintain democratic political institutions, ensuring democratic management of the government-owned industries; the communists preferred a dictatorship of the proletariat which

[18] Clement Attlee, *As It Happened* (New York: The Viking Press, Inc., 1954), pp. 228–29.

would have comprehensive control of these enterprises as well as of the rest of the economic life of the society.

The second basic economic tenet of socialism prior to 1950 was that the wealth of the society should be distributed equitably. This was to be accomplished by taxing inherited wealth heavily and by attaining a more equitable distribution of income through a sharply progressive income tax. As C. A. R. Crosland, a socialist and Member of the British Parliament put it:

The Socialist seeks a distribution of rewards, status, and privileges egalitarian enough to minimise social resentment, to secure justice between individuals, and to equalise opportunities; and he seeks to weaken the existing deep-seated class stratification, with its concomitant feelings of envy and inferiority, and its barriers to uninhibited mingling between the classes. This belief in socal equality, which has been the strongest ethical inspiration of virtually every socialist doctrine, still remains the most characteristic feature of socialist thought today.[19]

The third ingredient of a socialist economic system as socialists saw it prior to 1950 was government planning. Instead of allowing for the free play of private enterprise to make the basic economic decisions, socialists wanted these decisions made by the government on the basis of a coordinated and comprehensive economic plan. Once the plan was drawn up, the government would execute it by a comprehensive system of licensing, rationing, and allocation controls.

SOCIALISM AFTER 1950 / In this and the following chapter we shall be dealing extensively with ideas set forth by C. A. R. Crosland. We should like, therefore, to take pause and identify him.

Crosland, born in 1918, has been an active member of the British Labour Party since his Oxford days. He has served as a Member of Parliament from 1950 to 1955 and since October, 1959. During all of his active political life he has regarded himself as a socialist, although some of the more orthodox socialists would like to read him out of the movement. Although he is not a nominal leader of the Labour Party, he is considered an intellectual leader—at least, of one wing of the Party. In reviewing Crosland's latest book, *The Conservative Enemy*, for the *New Statesman*, George Lichtheim

---

[19] C. A. R. Crosland, *The Future of Socialism* (London: Jonathan Cape, 1956), p. 113.

accurately and succinctly described him as "the ablest and most persuasive spokesman of Labour's 'New Right.'" [20]

Like American parties, the British Labour Party is split into two wings, and no spokesman for one wing represents accurately the views of the other wing any more than Senator Goldwater speaks for Governor Rockefeller or Senator Thurmond for Senator Humphrey. Thus we offer Crosland's views not as representative of all British Socialists but rather because of their intrinsic worth and because a significant number of British Socialists subscribe to them.

You will note that we draw Crosland's comments from his book *The Future of Socialism* (1957), rather than from his more recent *The Conservative Enemy* (1962). We have done so because his views have not changed and the earlier book contains a more systematic and thorough explication of them.

The economic ideas of many socialists have undergone a startling change in the past decade. Doubtless, their experience as the governors in power in such countries as England, Sweden, Israel, and India among others has shattered some of their most sharply held beliefs. Significantly, many socialists are not so sure any longer that government ownership is desirable. For example, Crosland wrote in 1956:

The Labour Party having decided, rightly, to pay full compensation, the transfer of industries to state ownership does not have any large or immediate effect on the distribution of income. Over the long run there is, of course, a connection; but even in the long run other methods of redistribution are now seen to be simpler and more effective. As a determinant of relative shares in total income, the ownership of industrial property is less important than the level of employment, the behavior of prices, government controls (e.g. over rent or dividends), and above all taxation policy; and a determined government can restrict property incomes more easily than by the collectivisation of industry with full compensation. In addition, nationalisation has thrown up certain stubborn and largely unexpected problems which, so long as they remain unsolved, in any case make it impracticable to rely on public ownership as the main method of raising wages at the expense of property incomes.

. . . . .

This does not mean that nationalisation may not be justified on other grounds, nor that over the long period it has no influence of any kind on income-distribution, nor that the egalitarian objective to which

---

[20] *New Statesman*, November 30, 1962, p. 790.

it was directed has lost its relevance. It simply means that the ownership of the means of production . . . is no longer the *essential* determinant of the distribution of incomes; private ownership is compatible with a high degree of equality, while state ownership, as the Russian experience has demonstrated, may be used to support a high degree of inequality.[21]

Nehru, too, now feels that there is room for private enterprise in a socialist economy. He wrote that the national plan of a socialist economy "need not—and, indeed, should not—have rigidity. It need not be based on any dogma; but should rather take the existing facts into consideration. It may—and, I think, in present-day India it should—encourage private enterprise in many fields, though even that private enterprise must necessarily fit in with the national plan and have such controls as are considered necessary." [22]

The Social Democratic Party, which has been the major component of the coalition governing Sweden, in accordance with its declared policy allows private enterprise to continue in so far as it contributes to the public welfare. In 1957 the British Labour Party took much the same position when it resolved that the government should only take over industries after a public inquiry showed that they were inefficient. Nor has the British Labour Party, as a party, shown any inclination since that time to advocate a comprehensive and aggressive program of nationalization.[23] There is still a militant minority of party leaders and members who desire to push ahead with nationalization. It is of utmost significance that at this time, they cannot even get a majority of professing socialists to go along with them.

It is interesting that British and Swedish socialists have never tried to nationalize completely their nation's economies when they have been in power. For example, in Sweden the State owns only 1 per cent of all manufacturing capacity, cooperatives 4 per cent, and private enterprise 95 per cent. The 1 per cent is of real importance, however, for it includes among other things an iron and steel plant which produces one-third of Sweden's production in that important industrial field. In Britain, only about one-fourth of the means of production and distribution are owned by the state.

The following remarks of Crosland on the future of nationalization are illuminating:

---

[21] Crosland, *op. cit.*, p. 89.   [22] Nehru, *op. cit.*, p. 111.
[23] See Harold Wilson, "Wilson Defines British Socialism," *The New York Times Magazine*, September 15, 1963, p. 32.

But do we now simply go on, and in our next period in office take over the next five largest industries, and so on *ad infinitum?* Not many socialists would now definitely answer yes; and for the first time for a century there is equivocation on the Left about the future of nationalisation.

For this there are several reasons. The first and most obvious is that reality proved rather different from the blueprints. Some of the anticipated advantages did not materialise; while certain unexpected disadvantages emerged.[24]

In respect to the distribution of wealth, also, some socialists have had some second thoughts. Experience has taught them that a free people respond to material incentives more strongly than they had suspected. As Crosland put it:

All it seems possible to say in practice is (a) that people can work hard and contentedly for personal (or family) gain, (b) that people can work badly and discontentedly even when they are working for the common good, (c) that no doubt they work best of all when both motives are present, but (d) if it is desired, on moral grounds, to effect a general conversion from self-regarding to other-regarding motives, this will be hard to achieve, since it might require either a change in the basic "social character" or the creation of a largely novel institutional framework. This conclusion was of course reached at an early stage by the Soviet rulers, who quickly gave up the struggle and simply introduced the old "capitalist" incentives, under the new label of "Stakhanovitism" [a system for rewarding, with incentive pay and glory, especially productive workers], in an extreme and brutal version.[25]

Once it is recognized that material incentives are necessary, there is a tendency to make the economic rewards bigger and bigger. This tendency obviously runs counter to any idea of equalizing incomes. When the socialists were in power in England there was a wide disparity in the incomes of laborers and industry managers.

As for planning, here too, Crosland tells us the socialists have learned much:

This [planning] necessarily involves an intricate complex of licensing, rationing, and allocation controls; and these were increasingly seen to have serious drawbacks. They deny the consumer a free choice of goods and suppliers. They are highly unpopular, as was clearly shown by the public reaction to derationing. They involve an excessive growth of

---

[24] Crosland, *op. cit.*, p. 466.   [25] *Ibid.*, p. 109.

bureaucracy, with its concomitant dangers of petty tyranny, graft, and corruption.

And they are often economically inefficient. Not only do the planners often make mistakes, so that bottlenecks are created because the pro-duction budgets are not internally consistent; but there are also in prac-tice more inescapable weaknesses. Thus raw material allocations, being inevitably, for political reasons, non-discriminatory and therefore based on past performance, simply perpetuate the *status quo*, discourage new entry, and protect the less efficient firms from the competition of the more efficient. Price and investment controls (even if the former lead to no deterioration in quality), since they tend to be more effective the simpler and more essential the goods, often create a situation in which wages and profits are higher in the less essential than the more essential sectors of the economy; and resources are attracted in completely the wrong directions—from new housing to miscellaneous repair work, utility to non-utility textiles and so on. Many controls, moreover, are impossible to operate effectively once supplies become plentiful; they can be too easily circumvented, and a "grey" market develops (as happened at different times with commodities as various as steel and eggs). And in the end a detailed attempt to plan the output of different industries is bound to fail unless backed by direction of labour; and this no one was willing to countenance as a permanent measure.[26]

The present thinking of socialist leaders regarding planning is that there need not be a "detailed, overall government plan embracing every industry." Rather, "remaining severely empirical, the Govern-ment must stand ready first to intervene negatively to stop industry from acting manifestly against the public interest: secondly, and of far greater importance, to intervene positively to secure expansion— to search out the weak spots, especially in the basic industries, and concentrate on these with all the vigour at its command." [27] Prime Minister Nehru suggests, however, that in underdeveloped countries, a higher degree of planning is still necessary:

It is only through a planned approach on Socialist lines that steady [economic] progress can be attained, though even that will take time. . . .

Planning is essential for this because, otherwise, we waste our re-sources, which are very limited. Planning does not mean a mere collection of projects or schemes but a thought-out approach of how to strengthen the base and pace of progress so that the community advances on all fronts. In India we have a terrible problem of extreme poverty in certain

---

[26] *Ibid.*, pp. 500–501.   [27] *Ibid.*, p. 510.

large regions, apart from the general poverty of the country. We have always a difficult choice before us: whether to concentrate on production by itself in selected areas and favorable areas, thus for the moment rather ignoring poor areas, or try to develop the backward areas at the same time, so as to lessen the inequalities between regions. A balance has to be struck and an integrated national plan evolved.[28]

It is clear that traditional socialism is being so extensively modified as to require redefinition. In countries like England and Sweden, the approach of the socialists now differs very little from that of the modern capitalists. This fact has disturbed socialists all over the world and caused them to do much soul-searching about the real meaning of socialism. Articulations of this soul-searching stress that government ownership, equitable distribution of wealth, and rigid government planning were only the *means* which socialists thought they would use to achieve certain goals and that these *goals* rather than any means indicate the real meaning of socialism. The goals which are indicated are objectives like the elimination of unemployment and poverty, equal opportunity, concern for social welfare, and the rejection of competitive antagonism.[29] But these objectives are shared by governments other than socialist ones. Is it facetious to suggest that, perhaps unwittingly, the practicing socialists are becoming capitalists in their approach to economics?

THE EFFICACY OF TRADITIONAL SOCIALISM / Whatever the future of socialism, it is worthwhile to reflect on the efficacy of the economic system which socialists advocated before 1950, for there is much for us to learn from the recent experience of the socialists, particularly in Britain. Socialists indicate that they have learned that Madison was right about the nature of man and the early socialists wrong. To quote Crosland regarding the working man's reaction to nationalization:

The miners and railwaymen are in fact working for the public good as well as for themselves, and for an extremely urgent public good; and there are no shareholders or private profits to "expropriate" any of the fruits of their labour. Yet this appears to make only a limited psychological difference; and neither industry has a contented atmosphere. This might be a matter of scale and distance. The villager working on a community scheme, and building a new road for his village, can see the result with his own eyes, can see his own personal contribution

---

[28] Nehru, *op. cit.*, p. 111.   [29] Wilson, *op. cit.*

as being significant, and can see that his own community is in fact deriving benefit. The miner cannot see the total result of his efforts. . . .

Yet there might, for all we know, be quite a different explanation—that the average miner and railwayman are not sufficiently interested in the public good or the total result. It could plausibly be maintained that in these two industries, much more, for example, than in mass-production factories, the worker is exceptionally well aware of his personal role and contribution. . . . Yet this awareness, and such "social" incentive as may follow from it, may be outweighed by other incentives or emotions—local group solidarity, resentment over wages or conditions, dislike of the local management, disappointment (in the case of the railways) with the form of nationalisation and the performance of the Transport Commission; and so on.[30]

The socialists' resort to incentive systems was recognition that the ideal of "to each according to his needs and from each according to his ability" is not workable on a voluntary basis. The failures in detailed planning as discussed earlier point up our inability yet to understand fully complex economic processes and to make accurately the kinds of predictions necessary for such planning to be effective. Also, these failures illustrate, as Crosland suggests, that detailed planning leads to "an excessive growth of bureaucracy, with its comcomitant dangers of petty tyranny, graft, and corruption."

COMMUNISM

Unlike capitalism and socialism, communism is relatively easy to define. The communists have been doctrinaire and dogmatic about their economics. Consequently, the basic tenets of their economic system have remained virtually unchanged since Marx's day. As a matter of fact, among communists it is a serious "deviation" to depart very far from the economic ideas of Marx. True, communist nations have taken different paths in establishing communist economies. This is in accord with communist doctrine, which takes into account the fact that nations embark on the road to communism from different starting points. A moderately industrial state must take a different road to communism from that taken by a state with a highly agrarian economy. For example, the Chinese communist leaders found it advantageous for a few short years to permit a sub-

[30] Crosland, *op. cit.*, pp. 108–109.

stantial amount of private ownership of industry. Also, there are times when communist leaders regard it as necessary to backtrack from or soft-pedal the basic elements of their economic system for the moment. But they never waver from their firm belief that communist principles are valid and that they will ultimately prevail. Whenever they have felt compelled to modify these principles, communist leaders have not regarded the compulsion to modify as evidence that the principles were invalid. Rather they see the need for modification only as concessions to their people who have not yet reached the maturity and understanding required for living in the perfect and classless society.

As to economics, communism is based on three elements: (1) government ownership of *all* property, (2) equal distribution of the proceeds of labor, and (3) complete government control and planning of the economy. To be sure, these are much like the principles of early socialism. There are these essential differences, however: (1) the extent to which government owns, controls, and plans; (2) the political apparatus which constitutes the government—early socialists generally aspired to have democratic political institutions, while the communists want a dictatorship at least until the millennium arrives, and (3) the extent to which the communists have put the three basic propositions of communism into effect in countries which they control. In this connection it is interesting to note how Engels, the coauthor of the Communist Manifesto, distinguished between communism and socialism:

Yet, when it was written, we could not have called it a Socialist Manifesto. By Socialists, in 1847, were understood, on the one hand, the adherents of the various Utopian systems; (Owenites in England, Fourierists in France, both of them already reduced to the position of mere sects, and gradually dying out); on the other hand, the most multifarious social quacks, who, by all manners of tinkering, professed to redress, without any danger to capital and profit, all sorts of social grievances; in both cases men outside the working class movement, and looking rather to the "educated" classes for support. Whatever portion of the working class had become convinced of the insufficiency of mere political revolutions, and had proclaimed the necessity of a total social change, that portion, then called itself Communist. It was a crude, rough-hewn, purely instinctive sort of Communism; still, it touched the cardinal point and was powerful enough amongst the working class to produce the Utopian Communism, in France of Cabet, and in Germany of Weitling.

Thus, Socialism was, in 1847, a middle-class movement, Communism a working class movement. Socialism was on the Continent at least, "respectable"; Communism was the very opposite. And as our notion, from the very beginning, was that "the emancipation of the working class must be the act of the working class itself," there could be no doubt as to which of the two names we must take. Moreover, we have, ever since, been far from repudiating it.[31]

In November, 1957, communist leaders from Albania, Bulgaria, Hungary, Vietnam, East Germany, China, Korea, Mongolia, Poland, Rumania, Czechoslovakia, and the Soviet Union gathered together in Moscow and reaffirmed the economic bases of communism:

The meeting confirmed the identity of views of the Communist and Workers' parties on the cardinal problems of the Socialist revolution and Socialist construction. The experience of the Soviet Union and other Socialist countries has fully borne out the correctness of the Marxist-Leninist proposition that the processes of the Socialist revolution and the building of socialism are governed by a number of basic laws applicable in all countries embarking on a socialist course. These laws manifest themselves everywhere, alongside a great variety of historic national peculiarities and traditions which must by all means be taken into account.

These laws are: Guidance of the working masses by the working class, the core of which is the Marxist-Leninist party, in effecting a proletarian revolution in one form or another and establishing one form or other of the dictatorship of the proletariat; the alliance of the working class and the bulk of the peasantry and other sections of the working people; *the abolition of capitalist ownership and the establishment of ownership of the basic means of production; gradual Socialist reconstruction of agriculture; planned development of the national economy* aimed at building socialism and communism, at raising the standard of living of the working people; the carryng out of the Socialist revolution in the sphere of ideology and culture and the creation of a numerous intelligentsia devoted to the working class, the working people and the cause of socialism; the abolition of national oppression and the *establishment of equality* and fraternal friendship between the peoples, defense of the achievements of socialism against attacks by external and internal enemies; solidarity of the working class of the country in question with the working class of other countries, that is, proletarian internationalism [32] [italics supplied].

---

[31] Marx, *op. cit.*, pp. 317–18.
[32] *New York Times*, November 22, 1957. It is interesting to note that despite Engels' distinction between socialists and communists, many communists consider communism a special brand of socialism.

They agreed that "disregard of national peculiarities by the proletarian party inevitably leads to its divorce from reality, from the
masses and is bound to prejudice the cause of socialism." They made
it clear, however, that communists must not be carried away from
fundamentals: ". . . exaggeration of the role of these peculiarities
or departure, under the pretext of national peculiarities, from *the
universal Marxist-Leninist truth* on the Socialist revolution and the
Socialist construction is just as harmful to the Socialist cause" (italics
supplied).

Mindful of the frequent charge that they are too dogmatic and
of the efforts of some communists to deviate from the Marxist-
Leninist line, the assembled leaders said that they in truth "con-
demned dogmatism." Yet at the same time they observed that "the
main danger at present is revisionism or, in other words, right-wing
opportunism." And they ended up by dogmatically defending the
orthodox line: "Modern revisionism seeks to smear the great teach-
ings of Marxism-Leninism."

*How the Communists Implement
Their Economic Principles*
GOVERNMENT OWNERSHIP / *Industry.* Upon taking over the
government of any country, the communists have been quick to
wrest from private hands the means of industrial production and
distribution. Even in communist China, after several years of tem-
porizing with private ownership, the government has in recent years
moved swiftly to take over banking, foreign trade, and heavy industry. Having once taken over these enterprises, government rules
them with an iron hand. A good indication of this is the minor role
played by labor unions in the Soviet Union. Their role has been
described by one of the leading American experts on the Soviet
Union, Professor Merle Fainsod of Harvard University, in the following manner:

The Soviet trade unions are not bargaining units in the Western sense
of the term. They do not have the right to strike, and decisions on basic
wage rates, output norms, hours of labor and similar matters are a prerogative of government rather than of the trade unions. Such determinations on a national scale are made by the State Committee on Labor and
Wages, and the Central Council of Trade Unions plays chiefly a consult-
ing and advisory role. At lower levels, however, in the plants and factories where the problem arises of applying these general regulations,
there is provision for more active participation by the trade-union com-

mittees. Management is required to obtain their agreement in assigning workers to wage categories, in establishing work quotas, in introducing regulations on progressive piecework and bonus systems, and in determining other matters involved in wage administration. But the Regulations on the Rights of Factory, Plant, and Local Trade Union Committees approved in 1958 also made clear that such determinations must be "in accordance with existing standard regulations." The same regulations provided for a strengthening of the authority of the local trade-union committees in other respects. They were given the right to "participate" in working out production and financial plans of enterprises, to supervise the observance of labor legislation and collective agreements, to express their opinions on candidates nominated for management posts, and to veto discharges of workers and employees initiated by management. How effectively these rights are exercised is not easily ascertainable.[33]

Thus, despite elaborate pretenses of industrial democracy, the workers apparently have little real say as to their conditions of labor and wages or plans for the enterprise.

In communist countries, industry is a rigidly controlled enterprise with control shared by the managers and Party functionaries. Control commissions are set up by Party organizations in industrial and trade enterprises. In 1959, Khrushchev described the role these commissions are expected to play:

These commissions must keep a systematic check on the enterprises' timely fulfillment of their production quotas, state orders and deliveries of all the articles specified and their quality; they must also see to it that all the personnel of the enterprises strictly abide by state discipline and combat all manifestations of local selfish interest and a narrow departmental approach as harmful to statewide interests. They can lodge a protest against a decision taken by the management and report to Party and governmental bodies on any unlawful, wrong actions or decisions that are contrary to the law or Party and government decisions.[34]

Agriculture. Although communist governments have been able to communize industry swiftly, they have everywhere encountered difficulty in so doing with agriculture. As Professor Merle Fainsod aptly summed it up:

The peasantry, perhaps more than any other element in transitional societies, tends to be distrustful of change. The world of the peasant is

---

[33] Merle Fainsod, *How Russia Is Ruled* (Cambridge: Harvard University Press, 1963), pp. 519–20.
[34] Quoted in *ibid.*, pp. 515–16.

bounded by a profound attachment to the land. When he is landless or has only dwarf holdings, his revolutionary aspirations take the form of a hunger for land. When he is established on his own property, he obstinately resists being swept into the anonymity of the collective. Of all the major revolutionary transformations of the Soviet period, none was more difficult to effect than the collectivization of agriculture. Once achieved, the persistent efforts of the peasantry to evade its discipline presented the regime with problems of control and adjustment which have still to be satisfactorily resolved.

. . . . .

When the regime feels powerful enough to disregard peasant sentiment, opposition is brushed aside, and the Communist leadership ruthlessly imposes its will on the peasants. When it operates under the necessity of wooing peasant support or holding out greater incentives to stimulate output, concessions to the peasantry are forthcoming. Although the pendulum of policy has swung back and forth with the regime's changing assessment of its own position and needs, the ideological commitment is firmly to collectivism. In the words of the 1961 Party program, "The economic flowering of the collective-farm system creates the conditions for gradually bringing closer together collective-farm ownership and public ownership and in the long run for their merging in a single communist ownership." [35]

Thus, although communist leaders have traditionally made it clear that their ultimate objective in regard to agriculture is to have only large state-owned and state-operated farms, paralleling the organization of industry, they have in most countries under their control been willing to settle for a time on a system based upon the "collective farm," which is a curious mixture of state and private enterprise. This is not to imply that in those countries there are no state farms as such; there are state farms in most communist countries just as there are still small privately-owned and operated farms in some of them. But the great bulk of the agricultural activity in communist countries is carried on in collective farms. In the Soviet Union, however, there has been a dramatic increase in the number of state-owned farms at the expense of the collectives in recent years. According to Fainsod:

In 1953 kolkhozes [collectives] accounted for 89.5 per cent of the land sown to grain while the sovkhozes [state] tilled 8.7 per cent. By 1959 the kolkhoz share decreased to 66.8 per cent while the sovkhozes increased their proportion to 32 per cent.[36]

---

[35] *Ibid.*, p. 526.   [36] *Ibid.*, p. 558.

As Fainsod went on to indicate, "These statistics dramatized the determination of the regime to push the extension of state farming wherever it promised to be more productive."

The collective farm in communist countries is an association of farmers joined together to cultivate land leased to them in common and in perpetuity by the government and to raise livestock under rules and regulations set by the government. In the early days of communism, farmers joined collectives voluntarily, often with the encouragement of the government. Once the movement got under way, communist governments began to coerce farmers into joining collectives and into merging small collectives together.

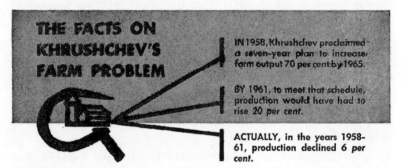

THE FACTS ON KHRUSHCHEV'S FARM PROBLEM

IN 1958, Khrushchev proclaimed a seven-year plan to increase farm output 70 per cent by 1965.

BY 1961, to meet that schedule, production would have had to rise 20 per cent.

ACTUALLY, in the years 1958-61, production declined 6 per cent.

SOURCE: U.S. Dept. of Agriculture. Reprinted from *U.S. News & World Report*, March 19, 1962, published at Washington. Copyright 1962, U.S. News & World Report, Inc.

In the collective as distinguished from the state farm, the individual farmer retains ownership in his homestead, small agricultural tools, and barnyard animals; the collective and not the state owns the larger tools and implements as well as the livestock. Each family is permitted to have a small plot for their own use, personal or commercial. Instead of all production being turned over to the state, the collective must deliver only specified amounts at prices set by the government. What the collective produces above and beyond the requirements it may use for distribution to its members or to sell. The income which a collective receives is divided up among its members roughly in proportion to the amount of work they did; the managerial group of the collective tend to get much larger shares, however.

Originally, a "town meeting" of the collective set policy for the

Troubles of Two Nations —

Too Much Food in U. S., Not Enough in Russia

IN U.S., farm efficiency is leaping forward. <u>Number of people supplied with food by each farm worker:</u>

1820		**4 PERSONS**
1870		**5 PERSONS**
1941		**12 PERSONS**
1955		**19 PERSONS**
1961 (est.)		**28 PERSONS**

IN RUSSIA, each farm worker supplies   **5 PERSONS**

THIS WAS THE U.S. RATIO IN 1870

U. S. FOOD is superabundant, piling up in storage.

RUSSIAN FOOD is barely sufficient. Farm program can't get off the ground.

FARMING engages 5.8 million American workers, 8.4 per cent of the total. Russia requires 48 million farm workers, 45 per cent of the total.

U. S., with a smaller population, has 5 times as many tractors as Russia, 4 times as many farm trucks, twice as many grain combines.

EFFICIENCY — output per manhour — has jumped 80 per cent on U. S. farms in just 12 years. Russian efficiency is less than a fourth that of U. S.

IN SHORT — Russia's Communist farming is nearly 100 years behind America's free-enterprise farming.

BASIC DATA: U.S. Dept. of Agriculture. Reprinted from *U.S. News & World Report*, October 23, 1961, published at Washington. Copyright 1961, U.S. News & World Report, Inc.

group and elected by democratic means managers who executed the policy. Today, the chairmen of the collectives are generally selected or approved by the Party and the members have no choice but to approve the selection.

The governors of the Soviet Union have learned the hard way that, as much as they abhor encouraging private enterprise in any way, shape, or form, attempts to communize agriculture lead to lower production. The farmer doggedly refuses to do his best unless he has some kind of material incentive like being able to share in the proceeds of production in excess of quota or having a little plot of ground which he may till for his own benefit after meeting his obligation to the collective.

In early 1958, the Chinese communist government embarked on an ambitious program designed to set up large agricultural communes in which "a few thousand to 10,000 peasant households merge their farm collectives into an organization that takes over all collective property as well as the small plots, tools, livestock and fowls the peasants have been permitted to keep individually." [37] Under the proposed system, the peasants would no longer distribute the income of the collective but would receive fixed wages. Significantly, most recent reports indicate that the government is adopting a go-slow policy because of peasant resistance. [38] In Poland, in recent years, the government has carried out a program of decollectivizing farms and allowing once more for private ownership on a large scale. The difficulties which communist governments have with agricultural production are illustrated in the newspaper article reproduced on the next two pages.

EQUAL DISTRIBUTION OF THE PROCEEDS OF LABOR / Communist leaders have long accepted the teaching of Marx that the proceeds of labor, the wealth of the society, *should* be divided on the basis of need among all the people who are working as hard as they can in whatever job they are performing for the state, need being determined by the size of each worker's family. But the communists have found that to obtain performance and to get people to take on the responsibility of top administrative posts they have

---

[37] Tillman Durdin, "Red China Slows Commune System," *New York Times*, September 28, 1958.
[38] *Ibid.* Also, Durdin, "On China Home Front: Major Reforms Begin," *New York Times*, September 28, 1958.

China Makes 'Tactical Retreat'

'Commune' system flops; 'small freedoms' offered

Second of two articles

By ROBERT HEWETT

Minneapolis Star and Tribune
Far East Correspondent

HONG KONG. Chinese Communist propaganda is making a big thing of the campaign to try to revive China's sagging farm output by putting the damper (temporarily) on the "commune" system and holding out material incentives for the peasants.

But two slogans repeated in the controlled press to the point of boredom show that the "relaxation" is not meant to get out of hand. The slogans: "Politics in Command."

"Large Plan, Small Freedoms."

The "freedoms" are indeed pitifully small, even by standards in rural China where the peasants have always had a hard life.

The "private plots" on which peasants are again permitted to raise vegetables, poultry and pigs for their own dinner table or for private sale are tiny. A Canton newspaper reported recently that the private plots in the South China province of Kwangtung range from about 14 feet square to 33 feet square for a farm family.

Men, women and older children are still required to put in full time raising primary crops such as grain, cotton or soybeans for the state on the fields of the collective farms. They can cultivate their private plots only in their spare time or on their days off —legally set at four days a month.

Rural trade fairs, the traditional markets of the peasants, were closed down in the Marxist "great leap forward" of 1958. The peasants staged a silent rebellion, marked by apathy rather than defiance, and now the fairs are permitted again.

This is the way the "small freedoms" work, as outlined recently in the Peking newspaper Kung-jen Jih-Pao:

"Side occupations carried on by the members' families are necessary supplements to the socialist economy. Members shall own and dispose of the farm produce and income from their private plots and private hills, from raising of domestic livestock and poultry like pigs, sheep, rabbits, chickens and ducks, from family handicrafts like knitting, tailoring, embroidery work, and from side occupations like fishing, hunting, silkworm breeding and bee-keeping.

"Except the farm produce which is on the list of state-planned purchase and marketing, all the other farm products may, after fulfilling the contracts signed with the state, be sold at the fairs."

Some idea of the twists and turns in the party line regarding these "vestiges of capitalism" can be obtained by careful reading of Communist Chinese newspapers which reach this British colony of Hong Kong; and by interviewing refugees and visitors from China.

Small as these "material incentives" are, the long-winded explanations given in the controlled press demonstrate that the Mao Tse-tung regime is chagrined at being forced by practical economic necessity to make even a tactical retreat on the march toward the Communist goal.

Another ever-present slogan held before the workers and peasants is: "To each according to his work, and more pay for more work."

When all China is finally organized into prosperous communes, party leaders explain in the press, then "the Communist consciousness of the masses will be fully aroused." On that Utopian day there will be no need for material incentives and there will come into play the dictum enunciated a century ago by Karl Marx: "From each according to his ability, and to each according to his needs."

The 1958 commune experiment flopped (although no Communist leader dares admit publicly even today that it failed) because Mao tried to force this egalitarian principle.

This has now been abandoned. Some idea of the flip-flop in the party line is shown by this extract from a Peking newspaper series on the need for incentives:

"Equal distribution . . . lends itself to capitalistic ways like loafing, speculation, idling and enjoying ready-made benefits."

What about the future? Informed foreign observers of China's chaotic farm situation believe the Mao regime will be forced by economic reality to make even more concessions—just as

Soviet Russia is doing—to stimulate peasant production.

This view is borne out by an article last month in the newspaper Ta-Kung Pao which, in a masterful piece of Communist understatement, said the party had "acquired rich experience" in the last few years. Commenting on the recent "discussions" by economists, the newspaper added:

"All agreed that the existence of trade at rural fairs was dictated by the political and economic conditions of the rural areas at the present stage and by the level of productive forces and the degree of consciousness of the people, and that such trade (rural fairs) would continue to exist for a considerable length of time."

In plain words, this means Mao and his Communist clique have learned by bitter experience that China's millions are not yet ready, willing and able to enter the Communist paradise. But they will keep pushing.

Robert Hewett in the *Minneapolis Star*, March 20, 1962. Copyright by *Minneapolis Star*. Reprinted by permission.

---

had to divide the proceeds in such a way as to provide material incentives. For neither medals, nor propaganda, worker glorification, nor force have proved as effective in the long run in obtaining performance as material incentives. They deny, however, that current practices invalidate the theory. They argue as did Marx that what ought-to-be can only come when the people are reoriented in their thinking. According to Marx:

> In a higher phase of Communist society, after the enslaving subordination of the individual to the division of labor shall have disappeared, and with it the antagonism between intellectual and manual labor, after labor has become not only a means of life but also the primary necessity of life; when, with the development of the individual in every sense, the productive forces also increase and all the springs of collective wealth flow with abundance—only then can the limited horizon of bourgeois right be left behind entirely and society inscribe upon its banner: "From each according to his abilities, to each according to his needs!" [39]

When the Soviet Union in the early 'thirties embarked on a comprehensive monetary-incentive system to the derision of Western

---

[39] Marx, *op. cit.*, p. 7.

Russians Complete Formation of 17 Major Economic Regions

Reorganization Aims at More Efficient Management of Vast Set-up—Panels Will Plan and Coordinate Output

By THEODORE SHABAD

Special to The New York Times

MOSCOW, Feb. 23—The Soviet Government announced today the completion of a reorganization of the country into seventeen major economic regions.

The revamping, which began last summer, represents a new attempt to find the most efficient system of managing a vast economy on a planned basis.

The seventeen regions replace thirteen planning areas used by the State Planning Committee for purposes of long-term development.

In contrast to the previous regional system, which was used mainly for statistical and planning operations, the new regions are headed by coordinating and planning councils.

Pravda, the Soviet Communist party newspaper, in announcing completion of the reorganization, published a map of the regions and reports on the initial work of the new councils.

Pyotr F. Lomako, deputy chairman of the party organization of the Russian Republic, disclosed that permanent staffs of 740 persons had been named for the ten regions established within the republic, the largest in the Soviet Union.

The Ukraine has been divided into three economic regions. The four remaining regions are made up, respectively, of the Baltic republics, the Transcaucasian republics, the Central Asian republics and Kazakhstan.

Two republics, Moldavia and Byelorussia, have not been included in the seventeen-region system and are under separate economic management. Their isolation has not been officially explained. It probably is related to the fact that their economies have little in common with those of adjoining areas.

Mr. Lomako said the Russian Republic's party agency, which is part of the national party's Central Committee, had appointed permanent deputy chairman of the ten councils within the republic. Similar officials were appointed for the seven other councils.

Mr. Lomako indicated that these deputies would be concerned with the day-to-day operations of council affairs. High regional party and government officials are expected to act as chairmen at council meetings on an ex-officio basis.

A complete list of the council's deputy chairmen, who presumably will play a powerful role in economic affairs, has not been made public.

Pravda identified Y. K. Ragozin as deputy chairman in the Central Region, around Moscow; A. A. Kuznetsov in the Northwest Region, around Leningrad, and I. P. Krasozov in the Dnieper-Donets Region of the Ukraine.

Mr. Ragozin was second secretary of the Moscow city party organization until last year. No information is available on the two others.

Latest Step in Campaign

The system of seventeen economic regions was announced in the Soviet economic newspaper, Ekonomicheskaya Gazeta, last May. Contrary to expectations, coordinating and planning councils for each region were not completed until January.

The formation of the regions and their councils is the latest step in a series of reorganizations of industrial management that began in 1957. In that year several dozen central ministries dealing with industry were abolished and their management functions were transferred to about 100 regional bodies for the administration of installations and construction projects within their areas.

Although the new system has its shortcomings, such as an emphasis on local interests at the expense of national aims, the official view is that regional management has paid off by smoother operation.

The existence of 100 management bodies produced certain problems of coordination and planning that the new councils are expected to solve. Each council will be responsible for the development of resources and the coordination of production of the regional management bodies under their jurisdiction.

Mr. Lomako conceded that it was too early to assess the councils' operations. Proposals have been made, he said, to appoint committees under the council to deal with such problems as specialization and subcontracting of industrial production, improved interregional transport ties, the effectiveness of capital investment and the distribution of manpower resources.

critics, Stalin explained that the incentives were needed to prepare the way for the transition from socialism to communism:

The principle of socialism is that in a socialist society each works according to his ability and receives articles of consumption, not according to his needs, but according to the work he performs for society. This means that the cultural and technical level of the working class is as yet not a high one, that the distinction between mental and manual labor still exists, that the productivity of labor is still not high enough to insure an abundance of articles of consumption, and, as a result, society is obliged to distribute articles of consumption not in accordance with the needs of its members, but in accordance with the work they perform for society.

Communism represents a higher stage of development. The principle of communism is that in a communist society each works according to his abilities and receives articles of consumption, not according to the works he performs, but according to his needs as a culturally developed individual. This means that the cultural and technical level of the working class has become high enough to undermine the basis of the distinction between mental labour and manual labour, that the distinction between mental labour and manual labour has already disappeared, and that productivity of labour has reached such a high level that it can provide an absolute abundance of articles of consumption, and as a result society is able to distribute these articles in accordance with the needs of its members.

Some people think that the elimination of the distinction between mental labor and manual labor can be achieved by means of a certain cultural and technical equalization of mental and manual workers by lowering the cultural and technical level of engineers and technicians, of mental workers, to the level of average skilled workers. That is absolutely incorrect. Only petty-bourgeois windbags can conceive communism in this way. In reality the elimination of the distinction between mental labor and manual labor can be brought about only by raising the cultural and technical level of the working class to the level of engineers and technical workers. It would be absurd to think that this is unfeasible. It is entirely feasible under the Soviet system, where the productive forces of the country have been freed from the fetters of capitalism, where labor has been freed from the yoke of exploitation, where the working class is in power, and where the younger generation of the working class has every opportunity of obtaining an adequate technical education.[40]

Evidently, the Soviet Union is still in the "socialist" stage and its leaders expect it to be so for some time to come, for emblazoned in the current Constitution is the provision:

The principle applied in the U.S.S.R. is that of socialism: "From each according to his ability, to each according to his work."

In keeping with the professed aim of eventual equalization of wealth, communist governments have made it impossible by law to inherit wealth and, consequently, to accumulate large family fortunes. Nevertheless, they have continued to permit wide disparities in earned income. As a matter of fact, disparities continue to grow, and some observers have pointed out that in the "classless society" there are greater class differences than in capitalist countries. Note the differences in income in the first table below. Add for good measure the fact that income taxes in the capitalist United States are relatively much higher for high incomes than in the Soviet Union. The second table below indicates that differences have remained relatively stable over a five year period.

The real significance of Soviet practice is that despite protestations about seeking eventual equality in the distribution of wealth, they evidently have not found it practical to do so. Nor is there any indication that they are getting closer to it as the years go by. Contrary to their doctrines, the experience in communist countries would seem to offer the best evidence that the communist ideal of "from each according to his ability" is not compatible with the nature of man.

[40] Joseph Stalin, *Leninism* (New York: International Publishers, 1942), p. 368. By permission of International Publishers Co., Inc.

PLANNING / The idea of government planning of the economy is so basic in the Soviet Union that it is provided for in the Constitution. Article 11 of that Constitution reads:

The economic life of the U.S.S.R. is determined and directed by the state national-economic plan, with the aid of increasing the public wealth, of steadily raising the material and cultural standards of the working people, of consolidating the independence of the U.S.S.R. and strengthening its defensive capacity.

HOW INCOMES VARY IN U.S.S.R.'S "CLASSLESS" SOCIETY *

Some sample weekly wages in rubles: (Official exchange rate: 4 rubles to $1. Actual value of ruble: about 12 to $1.)

Kindergarten teacher	104
Woman street cleaner	115
Sales girl	115
Unskilled worker	138
Secretary	185
Chauffeur	185
Taxi driver (including tips)	254
Construction worker (including bonus)	254
Experienced high-school teacher	300
Experienced doctor	323
Skilled mechanic	346
Factory foreman	392
Young engineer (including bonus)	392
Skilled instrument maker	462
Experienced engineer (including bonus)	577
Head buyer in large plant (including bonus)	738
Department-store manager	808
Professor	1,385
Dean of college	2,077
Manager of large plant (including bonus)	2,769

* This information, based on data collected inside the U.S.S.R. by Dr. Homer Dodge and Norton Dodge in May, 1955, appeared in *U.S. News & World Report* on July 8, 1955.

Actually, the governments of all communist countries devise master comprehensive plans for the economy; they are generally designated as Three or Five-Year Plans, depending on the number of years to be encompassed. An attempt is made to make it appear that all interested parties participate democratically in devising these plans. In practice, however, officials of the government make the important decisions. In addition to the master plans, annual plans are drawn up. The newspaper account of one such plan which appears on page 111 gives some indication of how elaborate government economic planning has become in the Soviet Union.

VARIATIONS IN EARNINGS OF RUSSIAN WORKERS

Monthly earnings, 1960 (in rubles) *

Scientist (academician)	8,000–15,000
Minister (head of Government ministry or department)	7,000
Opera star	†5,000–20,000
Professor (science)	6,000–10,000
Professor (medicine)	4,000– 6,000
Docent (assistant professor)	3,000– 5,000
Plant manager	3,000–10,000
Engineer	1,000– 3,000
Physician, head	950– 1,800
Physician, staff	850– 1,000
Teacher, high school	850– 1,500
Teacher, primary school	600– 900
Technician	800– 2,000
Worker, skilled	1,000– 2,500
Worker, semiskilled	600– 900
Worker, unskilled	270– 500

* The official rate of exchange, as fixed by the Soviet Government, is 4 rubles = US$1. The actual purchasing power of the ruble, however, is more accurately represented by the official tourist rate of exchange of 10 rubles for US$1.
† The top salary at the Bolshoi Theater has been reported as 5,000 rubles a month. Outside appearances increase the artist's income.

From Edmund Nash, "Purchasing Power of Workers in the U.S.S.R.," reprinted from *Monthly Labor Review*, April, 1960, United States Department of Labor, Bureau of Labor Statistics.

WHO GAINED MOST IN THE BOOM OF THE '50s

POPULATION
(millions)

	1950	1959	GAIN
WESTERN EUROPE	240	257	17 MILLION
UNITED STATES	152	179	27 MILLION
RUSSIA	182	212	30 MILLION

STEEL PRODUCTION
(millions of tons)

	1950	1959	GAIN
WESTERN EUROPE	56	101	45 MILLION
UNITED STATES	97	126	29 MILLION
RUSSIA	30	66	36 MILLION

ELECTRIC-POWER OUTPUT
(millions of kilowatt-hours)

	1950	1959	GAIN
WESTERN EUROPE	230	450	220 MILLION
UNITED STATES	390	789	399 MILLION
RUSSIA	90	264	174 MILLION

COAL PRODUCTION
(millions of tons)

	1950	1959	GAIN
WESTERN EUROPE	487	509	22 MILLION
UNITED STATES	560	420	-140 MILLION
RUSSIA	204	558	354 MILLION

PIG-IRON PRODUCTION
(millions of tons)

	1950	1959	GAIN
WESTERN EUROPE	42	72	30 MILLION
UNITED STATES	65	85	20 MILLION
RUSSIA	21	47	26 MILLION

An economy based on elaborate detailed plans must be controlled and policed. Obviously, individual managers in industry or agriculture cannot be permitted to deviate from the plan or to fail to produce what the plan requires, for deviation and failure may jeopardize the whole plan. Control is achieved through the allocation of materials, manpower, and money; the policing is done by the party representatives assigned to all large enterprises.

As pointed out earlier in our discussion of socialism, large-scale planning in a highly-complex industrial society is bound to be difficult and inefficient. The communists evidently are now discovering that this is true. In 1958, Mr. Wladyslaw Bienkowski, Minister of Education in communist Poland, had this to say in reference to the "highly centralized method of directing those few sections of economic life which were thought to be the only important ones":

It allowed the whole effort to be directed towards a few key problems, e.g. towards the creation of heavy industry. It was therefore possible in a short time to attain much bigger results than any average achieved in the past. Especially for the backward countries endowed with possibilities

GROSS NATIONAL PRODUCT

(billions)

	1950	1959	GAIN
WESTERN EUROPE	$141	$300	$159 BILLION
UNITED STATES	$285	$484	$199 BILLION
RUSSIA	$100	$200	$100 BILLION

INDUSTRIAL PRODUCTION

(1953=100)

	1950	1959	GAIN
WESTERN EUROPE	86	137	51
UNITED STATES	82	116	34
RUSSIA	69	170	101

AUTO PRODUCTION

(thousands)

	1950	1959	GAIN
WESTERN EUROPE	1,100	4,100	3 MILLION
UNITED STATES	6,700	5,600	-1.1 MILLION
RUSSIA	64	125	61 THOUSAND

HOME BUILDING

(thousands)

	1950	1959	GAIN
WESTERN EUROPE	1,150	1,900	750 THOUSAND
UNITED STATES	1,396	1,350	-46 THOUSAND
RUSSIA	U N K N O W N		

CEMENT PRODUCTION

(millions of tons)

	1950	1959	GAIN
WESTERN EUROPE	47	90	43 MILLION
UNITED STATES	42	63	21 MILLION
RUSSIA	11	43	32 MILLION

EXPORTS

(billions)

	1950	1959	GAIN
WESTERN EUROPE	$19.5	$43.0	$23.5 BILLION
UNITED STATES	$10.1	$17.6	$ 7.5 BILLION
RUSSIA	$ 1.8	$ 4.4	$ 2.6 BILLION

Note: Western Europe includes Austria, Belgium, Denmark, France, Germany, Italy, Luxembourg, Netherlands, Norway, Sweden, Switzerland, Portugal, and United Kingdom. Some of the figures shown above also include negligible amounts for other European countries.

SOURCE: United Nations; preliminary estimates by Organization for European Economic Co-operation; U.S. Government agencies. In some instances, part-year data for 1959 were projected for the full year by USN&WR Economic Unit. Reprinted from U.S. News & World Report, March 14, 1960, published at Washington. Copyright 1960, U.S. News & World Report, Inc.

for building up heavy industry, this method is the only one that can lead to the creation of adequate conditions for economic development. Nevertheless in the particular conditions pertaining in Poland this method, though it undoubtedly produced some positive results, brought about severe negative ones as well. It caused unevenness of economic development, with consequences to be seen not only in the living conditions of the people but also in disturbances of the development of even those privileged sectors of our economy.

On the other hand, the high degree of centralization which was a condition *sine qua non* of that method resulted in a reduction and paralysis of that normal social initiative which is, and should be, one of the main

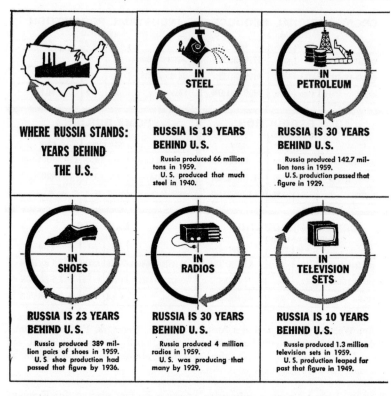

WHERE RUSSIA STANDS: YEARS BEHIND THE U.S.

IN STEEL

RUSSIA IS 19 YEARS BEHIND U.S.

Russia produced 66 million tons in 1959.
U. S. produced that much steel in 1940.

IN PETROLEUM

RUSSIA IS 30 YEARS BEHIND U.S.

Russia produced 142.7 million tons in 1959.
U. S. production passed that figure in 1929.

IN SHOES

RUSSIA IS 23 YEARS BEHIND U.S.

Russia produced 389 million pairs of shoes in 1959.
U. S. shoe production had passed that figure by 1936.

IN RADIOS

RUSSIA IS 30 YEARS BEHIND U.S.

Russia produced 4 million radios in 1959.
U. S. was producing that many by 1929.

IN TELEVISION SETS

RUSSIA IS 10 YEARS BEHIND U.S.

Russia produced 1.3 million television sets in 1959.
U. S. production leaped far past that figure in 1949.

driving forces of the universal—one might almost say organic—development of societies. Excess of red tape and atrophy of the social economic initiative are the two sides of the same coin with which we are paying for our successes in the key sectors of our economy. These factors caused progress in some sectors to be slower than it should have been from the purely economic point of view.[41]

As a consequence of the failure of centralized planning to achieve the results that communist leaders anticipated, planning is being more and more decentralized on a regional basis.

Appraisal of Communism as an Economic System

Just as the Russians have made startling advances in science, so have they made startling gains in the economic realm. They have increased production in both industry and agriculture at a rate far

---

[41] Wladyslaw Bienkowski, "The Political and Economic Situation in Poland Since October 1956," *International Affairs,* April, 1958, p. 140.

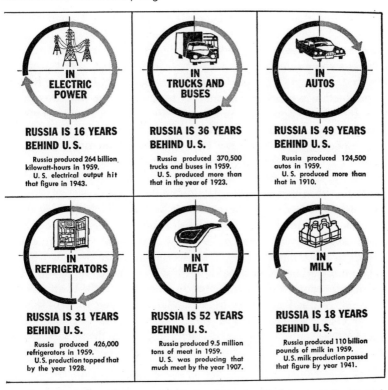

IN ELECTRIC POWER	IN TRUCKS AND BUSES	IN AUTOS
RUSSIA IS 16 YEARS BEHIND U. S.	**RUSSIA IS 36 YEARS BEHIND U. S.**	**RUSSIA IS 49 YEARS BEHIND U. S.**
Russia produced 264 billion kilowatt-hours in 1959. U. S. electrical output hit that figure in 1943.	Russia produced 370,500 trucks and buses in 1959. U. S. produced more than that in the year of 1923.	Russia produced 124,500 autos in 1959. U. S. produced more than that in 1910.
IN REFRIGERATORS	IN MEAT	IN MILK
RUSSIA IS 31 YEARS BEHIND U. S.	**RUSSIA IS 52 YEARS BEHIND U. S.**	**RUSSIA IS 18 YEARS BEHIND U. S.**
Russia produced 426,000 refrigerators in 1959. U. S. production topped that by the year 1928.	Russia produced 9.5 million tons of meat in 1959. U. S. was producing that much meat by the year 1907.	Russia produced 110 billion pounds of milk in 1959. U. S. milk production passed that figure by year 1941.

Note: The higher production of U.S. is achieved with fewer people. Russia's smaller output must be shared by more people.

Source: Russian production from Soviet publications. U.S. production from U.S. Dept. of Agriculture, U.S. Dept. of Commerce, and various private studies. Reprinted from *U.S. News & World Report*, May 2, 1960, published at Washington. Copyright 1960, U.S. News & World Report, Inc.

surpassing that of the United States, the chief exponent of capitalism. This fact has been the basis for their comparison of capitalism with communism, aimed at showing the superiority of communism over capitalism. But such a comparison should be taken with a large grain of salt. For one thing, it is easier to have a greater rate of increase where a nation starts from a low rate of production. Every student knows that it is relatively easier to improve a midterm grade of 50 than a midterm grade of 90. The communists had a longer way to go toward reaching high levels of production.

Compare the actual production figures of the two countries and you will find that the Soviet Union is far behind the United States. Remember, too, that the Soviet Union has a larger population and greater natural resources; with an equally efficient economic system, at some point the Soviet Union should be able to out-produce the United States. True, the United States had a big lead over Russia in production when the communists took over. But that was more than forty years ago. How much more time should the Russians be allowed before we can make fair comparisons of the effectiveness of our respective systems on the basis of total production? And note from the charts on the preceding pages the differences.

However measured, Soviet accomplishments in raising production have been considerable. Undoubtedly, a good part of the accomplishment is due to the economic system which enables them to be single-minded and ruthless in dealing with their own citizens. The Russian consumer does not hold the exalted position of his counterpart in the United States. The government there decides what is to be produced in the national interest without much regard to what the people want. Consequently, production gains in the Soviet Union have not resulted in a very high standard of living for its citizens. Victor Cohn, science reporter for the *Minneapolis Tribune,* made this pertinent observation upon returning from the Soviet Union several years ago:

> In the shadow of the Kremlin, in the wake of the sputniks, walks a woman out of the 19th century. She wears a dirty smock over a torn dress, a faded kerchief around her head; heavy, sagging cotton stockings; worn, lopsided shoes.
>
> Her face is lined and tired. Her hair straggles. Her skin is leathery. Her eyes are hard and lifeless. She is sweeping the street with a rude straw broom. She is maybe 32 years old.
>
> Russian workers today work harder and longer than almost any other "modern" industrial workers—so they eat a simple cabbage-bread-meat (not too much meat) diet, live in an average 46 square feet of space per human being, wear shabby clothes.[42]

SELECTED BIBLIOGRAPHY

CLEMENT ATTLEE, *As It Happened* (New York: The Viking Press, Inc., 1954).

---

[42] Victor Cohn, "The Year of the Sputnik," *Minneapolis Morning Tribune,* October 6, 1958.

CLEMENT ATTLEE, *The Labour Party in Perspective* (London: Victor Gollancz, Ltd., 1949).

C. A. R. CROSLAND, *The Conservative Enemy* (New York: Schocken Books, Inc., 1962).

C. A. R. CROSLAND, *The Future of Socialism* (London: Jonathan Cape, 1956).

WILLIAM EBENSTEIN, *Fascist Italy* (New York: American Book Company, 1939).

WILLIAM EBENSTEIN, *The Nazi State* (New York: Farrar, Straus & Cudahy, Inc., 1943).

MERLE FAINSOD, *How Russia Is Ruled* (Cambridge: Harvard University Press, 1963).

KARL MARX, *Capital, The Communist Manifesto, and Other Writings,* Max Eastman, ed. (New York: The Modern Library, Inc.).

PAUL SAMUELSON, *Economics* (New York: McGraw-Hill Book Co., Inc., 5th ed., 1961).

JOSEPH A. SCHUMPETER, *Capitalism, Socialism and Democracy* (New York: Harper & Brothers, 1947).

THE MARRIAGE OF POLITICAL
AND ECONOMIC SYSTEMS

4.

Thus far we have roughly classified the possible political systems into two major categories, democracy and authoritarianism; likewise, we have divided the economic systems into two broad categories, private ownership and government ownership. Employing these classifications, there are four possible combinations of economic and political systems.

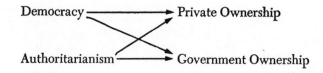

Democracy ⟶ Private Ownership

Authoritarianism ⟶ Government Ownership

In short, political democracy can be paired with either a system of private ownership or a system of government ownership. An authoritarian government can operate with either economic system. Proof of the pudding is the fact that we have actually seen all four of the combinations in practice. The United States represents a marriage between political democracy and a private ownership economy. Democratic socialism as practiced in Britain, Sweden, and India can be said to be a combination of democracy with a government economy, even though government ownership has not been extended to all areas of the economy. Nazi Germany and fascist Italy were good examples of authoritarian political systems combined with private ownership economies, and the Soviet Union and communist China are classic examples of authoritarian political systems married to economic systems of government ownership.

WHICH ECONOMIC SYSTEM IS
COMPATIBLE WITH POLITICAL DEMOCRACY?

Not all marriages are happy and successful. The mere fact that a marriage exists is no proof that it is happy and successful. Only a marriage where the partners are compatible can in the long run be truly satisfactory. So it is with the marriage of political and economic systems. It stands to reason that people who have strived for and achieved political democracy because they deeply believe in certain values will not long abide an economic system which does not square with those values. This is not to say that there is such a thing as "economic democracy"—although it is sometimes asserted. "Democracy," as we have seen earlier, is a term which describes political arrangements; it has no generally accepted or understood meaning in respect to economics. But to be compatible with political democracy an economic system must be predicated on the same propositions on which political democracy is based: (1) that the individual is the highest value; (2) that people are inherently equal; and (3) that the individual should be allowed the widest latitude of freedom consistent with the freedom of others. In general, there is agreement among democrats, on what each of the propositions means as applied to economics. The first proposition means that the economy should be operated for the benefit of the many and not the few, that it should give the highest standard of living possible to society as a whole, and that no one should be permitted to exploit other human beings. As for the second proposition, that people are equal, no democrat urges that this means that every one should earn the same salary or that there should be rotation in jobs so that everyone is a worker or manager in turn. Rather, democrats of both liberal and conservative bent have defined this proposition to mean that there should be equality of opportunity. For example, President Franklin D. Roosevelt in his famous "Four Freedoms Address" said:

For there is nothing mysterious about the foundations of a healthy and strong democracy. The basic things expected by our people of their political and economic systems are simple. They are:
    Equality of opportunity for youth and for others.

Jobs for those who can work.

Security for those who need it.

The ending of special privilege for the few.

The preservation of civil liberties for all.

The enjoyment of the fruits of scientific progress in a wider and
constantly rising standard of living.

It is significant that the only "equality" Roosevelt speaks of is
"equality of opportunity" and that it heads his list of "basic things
expected by our people." The conservative President Herbert Hoover
was wont to stress the same points:

Equality of opportunity is the right of every American—rich or poor,
foreign or native-born, irrespective of faith or color. It is the right of every
individual to attain that position in life to which his ability and character
entitle him. By its maintenance we will alone hold open the door of
opportunity to every new generation, to every boy and girl. It tolerates
no privileged classes or castes or groups who would hold opportunity as
their prerogative. Only from confidence that this right will be upheld can
flow that unbounded courage and hope which stimulate each individual
man and woman to endeavor and to achievement. The sum of their
achievement is the gigantic harvest of national progress.

This ideal of individualism based upon equal opportunity to every
citizen is the negation of socialism. It is the negation of anarchy. It is the
negation of despotism. It is as if we set a race. We, through free and universal education, provide the training of the runners; we give to them an
equal start; we provide in the Government the umpire of fairness in the
race. The winner is he who shows the most conscientious training, the
greatest ability, and the greatest character. Socialism bids all to end the
race equally. It holds back the speedy to the pace of the slowest. Anarchy
would provide neither training nor umpire. Despotism picks those who
should run and those who should win. . . .

Equality of opportunity is a fundamental principle of our nation.
With it we must test all our policies. The success or failure of this principle is the test of our Government.

The democrat of socialist persuasion would take issue with
Hoover's interpretation of what the socialists are seeking. The
socialists do not deny the importance of equality of opportunity. As
Crosland puts it:

The conclusion must be that in Britain equality of opportunity and social
mobility, though they lead to the most admirable distribution of intelligence, are not enough. They need, not to be played down, as some
sociologists would have us do, but to be combined with measures, above

all in the educational field, to equalise the distribution of rewards and privileges so as to diminish the degree of class stratification, the injustice of large inequalities, and the collective discontents which come from too great a dispersion of rewards. The limited goal is not, from a socialist point of view, sufficient.[1]

Although socialists, in Hoover's figure of speech, do want to see the race end up fairly close, they do not insist that everyone end up in a dead heat. Crosland again:

No Socialist (except for Shaw, and he not in later life) has disputed the need for a degree of inequality here, both because superior talent deserves some rent of ability, and because otherwise certain kinds of work, or risk, or burdensome responsibility will not be shouldered. Thus one should pay differentially high rewards to the artist, the coalminer, the innovating entrepreneur, and the top executive. But it is not clear that these considerations justify the present pattern of work-rewards, either in principle (that is, with respect to the overall spread from top to bottom) or in practice (that is, with respect to whether the right people are receiving the higher and lower incomes).[2]

As to the meaning of the third proposition, that the individual should enjoy the widest latitude of "freedom" possible in the economic sphere, there is disagreement on many of the specifics. Nonetheless there is substantial agreement on the basic elements which constitute "freedom."

Most democrats agree that people should have the opportunity to choose their jobs and callings except where the exercise of choice might jeopardize the well-being of others. Obviously, the man who has not acquired the necessary training should not be permitted to practice medicine. Too, there are times when the community may deem it wise to restrict the number of people engaged in a particular activity like selling liquor. There is also a practical limit to the number of people who can do particular jobs in society. If everyone in the United States decided he wanted to be a farmer or to run a grocery store, we would have an impossible situation. But within these practical limits an economic system to be compatible with political democracy must permit a wide latitude of choice of occupation. Perhaps the converse, that no one should be coerced to work at something he does not want to do, is even more important to political democrats. And even though it is practically impossible to permit

[1] Crosland, *The Future of Socialism,* p. 237.
[2] *Ibid.,* pp. 210–11.

everyone to pursue work of his choice, it does not follow that everyone must be assigned a job without consideration of personal preference.

If a young lady turns down nine suitors in order to marry number ten, we do not regard it as an unfair restriction on the freedom of choice of the nine who are turned down. By the same token, free men would not accept the alternative of assigning brides to the nine rejected suitors, but rather allow them to seek brides freely from among the remaining eligible ladies. In the same fashion democrats recognize practical limits to the freedom of choice of jobs, but find intolerable an economic system which eliminates all choice.

Other basic elements of freedom in the economic sphere on which democrats agree are (1) the opportunity to bargain over salaries and wages, (2) the opportunity to choose among employers, (3) the opportunity to work in the geographical area of the individual's choice, (4) the freedom of the individual to spend his net income (income after taxes) on those items which he chooses, and (5) the right to save and accumulate his money as well as to spend it.

Each of us can compile an additional list of items which we as individuals regard as basic to freedom in the economic sphere, but these would find no general agreement even among democrats. A good example is the question involved in the "right to work" controversy in the United States. Some believe that a man should be free to join or not to join a union. Others feel that to accord a working man such a choice would result in the demise of unions and consequently the real loss of freedom to the worker.

Despite the fact that there is no complete agreement as to all the elements of an economic system which democrats would find compatible with political democracy, as has been demonstrated, there is substantial agreement on the basic propositions. But it is one thing to determine the basic principles on which an economy must be based and quite another to determine the mechanics of a system which will best achieve those principles in a highly complex modern state. As a matter of fact, there has been real controversy for over one hundred years as to whether or not these principles are better achieved where government does or does not play a big part in the direction of the economy. Representative of the two schools of thought are Presidents Franklin D. Roosevelt and Herbert Hoover.

Roosevelt felt that only by a large measure of government control of the economy would it be possible to enhance the individual's worth, establish equality of opportunity, and provide for a wide measure of individual freedom. He saw as the alternative to government intervention in the economy, control of the economy by corporate enterprises which threatened the values most precious to democrats.

Just as freedom to farm has ceased, so also the opportunity in business has narrowed. It is still true that men can start small enterprises, trusting to native shrewdness and ability to keep abreast of competitors; but area after area has been preempted altogether by the great corporations, and even in the fields which still have no great concerns, the small man starts under a handicap. The unfeeling statistics of the past three decades show that the independent business man is running a losing race. Perhaps he is forced to the wall; perhaps he cannot command credit; perhaps he is "squeezed out" . . . by highly organized corporate competitors, as your corner grocery man can tell you. Recently a careful study was made of the concentration of business in the United States. It showed that our economic life was dominated by some six hundred odd corporations who controlled two-thirds of American industry. Ten million small business men divided the other third. More striking still, it appeared that if the process of concentration goes on at the same rate, at the end of another century we shall have all American industry controlled by a dozen corporations, and run by perhaps a hundred men. Put plainly, we are steering a steady course toward economic oligarchy, if we are not there already.

Clearly, all this calls for a re-appraisal of values. A mere builder of more industrial plants, a creator of more railroad systems, an organizer of more corporations, is as likely to be a danger as a help. The day of the great promoter or the financial Titan, to whom we granted anything if only he would build, or develop, is over. Our task now is not discovery or exploitation of natural resources, or necessarily producing more goods. It is the soberer, less dramatic business of administering resources and plants already in hand, of seeking to reestablish foreign markets for our surplus production, of meeting the problem of under-consumption, of adjusting production to consumption, of distributing wealth and products more equitably, of adapting existing economic organizations to the service of the people. The day of enlightened administration has come.

Just as in older times the central Government was first a haven of refuge, and then a threat, so now in a closer economic system the central and ambitious financial unit is no longer a servant of national desire, but a danger. I would draw the parallel one step farther. We do not think because national Government had become a threat in the 18th century that therefore we should abandon the principle of national Government. Nor today should we abandon the principle of strong economic units called corporations, merely because their power is susceptible of easy abuse. In other times we dealt with the problem of an unduly ambitious central Government by modifying it gradually into a constitutional democratic Government. So today we are modifying and controlling our economic units.

As I see it, the task of Government in its relation to business is to assist the development of an economic declaration of rights, an economic constitutional order. This is the common task of statesman and business man. It is the minimum requirement of a more permanently safe order of things.

On the other hand, Herbert Hoover saw government intervention in economic affairs as the primary threat to the cherished values of the political democrat.

The President of the United States [Roosevelt] on January 6, 1941, stated that we seek "everywhere in the world" the four old freedoms: freedom of speech and expression, freedom of religion, freedom from fear, freedom from want.

Soon thereafter I called attention to the fact that there is a Fifth Freedom—economic freedom—without which none of the other four freedoms will be realized.

I have stated many times over the years that to be free, men must choose their jobs and callings, bargain for their own wages and salaries, save and provide by private property for their families and old age. And they must be free to engage in enterprise so long as each does not injure his fellowmen. And that requires laws to prevent abuse. And when I use the term "Fifth Freedom," I use it in this sense only, not in the sense of laissez-faire or economic exploitation. Exploitation is the negation of freedom. The Fifth Freedom does not mean going back to abuses.

Laws to prevent men doing economic injury to their fellows were universal in civilized countries long before the First World War. In the United States, for example, the State and Federal Governments had established regulation of banks, railroads, utilities, coinage; prevention of combinations to restrain trade; government support to credit in times of stress; public works; tariffs; limitations on hours of labor and in other directions.

The key of such government action to economic freedom is that government must not destroy but promote freedom. When governments exert regulation of economic life, they must do so by definite statutory rules of conduct imposed by legislative bodies that all men may read as they run and in which they may have at all times the protection of the courts. No final judicial or legislative authority must be delegated to bureaucrats, or at once tyranny begins.

When Government violates these principles, it sooner or later weakens constitutional safeguards of personal liberty and representative government.

When Government goes into business in competition with citizens, bureaucracy always relies upon tyranny to win. And bureaucracy never develops that competence in management which comes from the mills of competition. Its conduct of business inevitably lowers the living standards of the people. Nor does bureaucracy ever discover or invent. A Millikan, Ford, or Edison never came from a bureaucracy.

And inherent in bureaucracy is the grasping spirit of more and more power. It always resents criticism and sooner or later begins directly or indirectly to limit free speech and free press. Intellectual and spiritual freedom will not long survive the passing of economic freedom. One of the illusions of our time is that we can have totalitarian economics and the personal freedoms. Ten nations on the Continent of Europe tried it and wound up with dictators and no liberty.

Time and experience has demonstrated that both of our presidents were right. Too much government as well as too little government control of the economy makes for an economic system which is incompatible with political democracy.

The American Experience with Too Little Government in Economics

As Roosevelt pointed out when the economy was relatively free from government control and regulation in the late nineteenth and early twentieth centuries, the inevitable result was the concentration of wealth and power in the hands of a few. Just as inevitably, this concentration of private power led to abuses, attesting further the validity of Lord Acton's famous aphorism that "power corrupts and absolute power corrupts absolutely." Even Hoover, an ardent protagonist against too much government in the economic sphere, recognized that "laissez faire" was not the answer either. He emphasized, as we have seen, that his "Fifth Freedom" did not mean returning to the abuses Roosevelt had catalogued. In short, where there was too little government, the values of democrats did not prevail in the economic sphere. The consequence of the incompatibility between the political and economic systems was bitterness and agitation for change.

The British Experience with Too Much
Government in Economics

Reacting to the abuses of laissez-faire economics, the British, after World War II, went much further than the United States ever has toward government control of the economy. Under the Labour government they embarked on a program of nationalization of industry and detailed government planning. As indicated earlier, with remarkable candor, some British socialists for a decade have been assessing the Labour Government's experience in the postwar period. Their assessments offer information of real importance to Americans. Consequently, it is surprising that they have not gained wider currency. The sum and substance of these assessments is that Britain went too far in the direction of government controls, too far in the sense that the experiment ceased to promote democratic values. For example, recall what Crosland wrote in respect to nationalization:

> But do we now simply go on, and in our next period in office take over the next five largest industries, and so on *ad infinitum?* Not many socialists would now definitely answer yes; and for the first time for a century there is equivocation on the Left about the future of nationalisation.
>
> For this there are several reasons. The first and most obvious is that the reality proved rather different from the blueprints. Some of the anticipated advantages did not materialise; while certain unexpected disadvantages emerged.

> · · · · ·

> A higher working-class standard of living, more effective joint consultation, better labour relations, a proper use of economic resources, a wider diffusion of power, a greater degree of co-operation, or more social and economic equality—none of these now primarily require a large-scale change in ownership for their fulfilment; still less is such a change a *sufficient* condition of their fulfilment.[3]

Observation of Britain's experience encouraged Crosland to conclude that nationalization was not the answer.

> But we want not only a larger stake in industry for the State, but also a wide diffusion of property amongst individuals. We should therefore welcome effective profit-sharing, and the indirect diffusion which goes with the growth of pension funds, workers' share banks, educational

[3] *Ibid.,* p. 466 and p. 475.

foundations, and charitable trusts. The objective is not wholly to destroy private ownership, but to alter its distribution.

The ideal (or at least my ideal) is a society in which ownership is thoroughly mixed-up—a society with a diverse, diffused, pluralist, and heterogeneous pattern of ownership, with the State, the nationalised industries, the Co-operatives, the Unions, Government financial institutions, pensions funds, foundations, and millions of private families all participating. Since this is still a long way off, we need heavy taxation to limit profits and dividends. And it may be an unpopular solution amongst the traditionalists of the Left, who still want . . . the steady creation of State monopolies.[4]

Another well-known British socialist reiterated this theme when he wrote: "The main task of socialism today is to prevent the concentration of power in the hands of *either* industrial management *or* the state bureaucracy—in brief, to distribute responsibility and so to enlarge freedom of choice." [5]

The significance of Crosland's remarks lies in his rejection of the desirability of extensive nationalization. It is significant, too, that the British Labour Party has ceased pressing for more nationalization.

Regarding extensive government planning in the economic sphere, Crosland wrote:

. . . no one of any standing now believes the once-popular Hayek thesis that any interference with the market mechanism must start us down the slippery slope that leads to totalitarianism. This was an unplausible enough view, in a British context, even when it was first advanced; it has been thoroughly discredited now that we have experienced a decade of varying degrees of government control, with no sign of a weakening of our democratic fibre.

Socialist views on planning have been similarly modified. The pre-war argument, based as it was on the combination of manifest inefficiency and glaring inequality displayed by the capitalism of the 1930s, has in any case lost much of its force in the expansionist full employment economy and the Welfare State of the 1950s. And the extreme post-war argument has also fallen rather out of fashion. This was based on a different set of considerations, relating primarily to the dollar shortage and the balance of payments, and the apparent need to allocate resources by detailed physical controls if social justice and external solvency were to be combined in a siege economy. The change in opinion is due partly to

[4] *Ibid.*, p. 496.
[5] R. H. S. Crossman, "Towards a Philosophy of Socialism," in Crossman (ed.), *New Fabian Essays* (London: Turnstile Press, 1952), p. 27.

the easing of the world economic situation as the post-war crisis years gave way to more normal conditions, and in particular as the American economy came to bely the worst fears expressed about it just after the war: but mainly to a general disillusionment with the whole notion of trying to control short-term production decisions from Whitehall through a detailed budget of production.

Crosland then went on to make the following points which were cited earlier but bear repetition in the present context:

This necessarily involves an intricate complex of licensing, rationing, and allocation controls; and these were increasingly seen to have serious drawbacks. They deny the consumer a free choice of goods and suppliers. They are highly unpopular, as was clearly shown by the public reaction to derationing. They involve an excessive growth of bureaucracy, with its concomitant dangers of petty tyranny, graft, and corruption.

And they are often economically inefficient. Not only do the planners often make mistakes, so that bottlenecks are created because the production budgets are not internally consistent; but there are also in practice more inescapable weaknesses. Thus raw material allocations, being inevitably, for political reasons, non-discriminatory and therefore based on past performance, simply perpetuate the *status quo,* discourage new entry, and protect the less efficient firms from the competition of the more efficient. Price and investment controls (even if the former lead to no deterioration in quality), since they tend to be more effective the simpler and more essential the goods, often create a situation in which wages and profits are higher in the less essential than in the more essential sectors of the economy; and resources are attracted in completely the wrong directions—from new housing to miscellaneous repair work, utility to non-utility textiles, and so on. Many controls, moroever, are impossible to operate effectively once supplies become plentiful; they can be too easily circumvented, and a "grey" market develops (as happened at different times with commodities as various as steel and eggs). And in the end a detailed attempt to plan the output of different industries is bound to fail unless backed by direction of labour; and this no one was willing to countenance as a permanent measure.

There has thus been, on both sides, a declining tendency to take up extreme positions; and the issue of planning (as opposed to the objectives of planning) is not now one of the fundamental differences between Left and Right. Naturally important differences of emphasis remain, productive of much political heat. But generally the issue now is not whether, but how much and for what purpose, to plan.[6]

---

[6] Crosland, *op. cit.,* pp. 500–501.

At an earlier time, Crosland asserted: "Within the framework of overall government planning, the proper way to make the private sector responsive to the needs of the community is to make it competitive. *The failure to do so was perhaps the greatest single failure of the post-1945 Labour Administration*" [7] (italics supplied).

Judging from the British socialists' assessment of their recent experience, too much government is as antipathetic to democratic values as too little government.

The Pertinence of Recent American Experience

During the New Deal, our national government embarked upon a studied policy of increasing government control over the economy. Liberals of the day felt that our political rights were not endangered by such an extension of government power. They rationalized that a distinction could be made between the economic and political spheres and that government intervention in the economic sphere was permissible whereas it was not permissible in the political realm. Liberals on the Supreme Court even supplied a constitutional basis for making such a distinction, the "preferred freedoms" doctrine. They argued that certain freedoms, specifically those enumerated in the First Amendment, held a preferred place in our scheme of things. This preferred position was justified by two lines of argument; first, the language of the First Amendment which in absolute language, not duplicated in respect to economic rights, forbids Congress from abridging free speech, press, assembly, and religion ("Congress shall make no law . . ."); and second, that these liberties are so essential for the maintenance of a democratic political system that they cannot be abridged without doing irreparable harm to the system itself, whereas freedom in the economic sphere could be limited by government without subverting political democracy. The best statement of the preferred freedoms doctrine is contained in the opinion of Justice Wiley Rutledge in *Thomas v. Collins* (1945):

> The case confronts us again with the duty our system places on this Court to say where the individual's freedom ends and the State's power begins. Choice on that border, now as always delicate, is perhaps more so *where the usual presumption supporting legislation is balanced by the preferred place given in our scheme to the great, the indispensable*

[7] Crosland, "The Transition from Capitalism," in *New Fabian Essays*, p. 64.

democratic freedoms secured by the First Amendment. That priority gives these liberties a sanctity and sanction not permitting dubious intrusions. And it is the character of the right, not of the limitation, which determines what standard governs the choice.

For these reasons any attempt to restrict those liberties must be justified by clear public interest, threatened not doubtfully or remotely, but by clear and present danger. *The rational connection between the remedy provided and the evil to be curbed, which in other contexts might support legislation against attack on due process grounds, will not suffice.* These rights rest on firmer foundation. Accordingly, whatever occasion would restrain orderly discussion and persuasion, at appropriate time and place, must have clear support in public danger, actual or impending. Only the gravest abuses, endangering paramount interests, give occasion for permissible limitation [italics supplied].

Some members of the present Supreme Court, typified by Justice Black, still make this distinction:

Unless state legislatures have power to make distinctions that are not plainly unreasonable, then the ability of the states to protect their citizens by regulating business within their boundaries can be seriously impaired. I feel it necessary to express again my objection to the use of general provisions of the Constitution to restrict narrowly state power over state economic affairs.

I think state regulation should be viewed quite differently where it touches or involves freedom of speech, press, religion, petition, or other specific safeguards of the Bill of Rights. It is the duty of this Court to be alert to see that these constitutionally preferred rights are not abridged.[8]

From the advent of the New Deal to World War II, liberals viewed the major problems of our society as economic in nature. They saw a need for more and more government intervention in the economic sphere to solve these problems. World War II accelerated the development of more government intervention. War by its very nature requires a large measure of governmental direction in the lives of the people of a nation. In this period of the 1930's and 1940's, when liberals regarded the kind of government intervention that was taking place as desirable, the idea of government intervention was being exalted. In his Annual Message to Congress in 1936, Franklin D. Roosevelt said:

In March, 1933, I appealed to the Congress and to the people . . . in a new effort to restore power to those to whom it rightfully belonged.

---

[8] Dissent of Justice Black in *Morey v. Doud*, 354 United States 457, 471 (1957).

The response to that appeal resulted in the writing of a new chapter in the history of popular government. You, the members of the legislative branch, and I, the Executive, contended for an established new relationship between government and people.

What were the terms of that new relationship? They were an appeal from the clamor of many private and selfish interests, yes, an appeal from the clamor of partisan interest, to the ideal of public interest. Government became the representative and the trustee of the public interest. Our aim was to build upon essentially democratic institutions, seeking all the while the adjustment of burdens, the help of the needy, the protection of the weak, the liberation of the exploited and the genuine protection of the people's property.

It goes without saying that to create such an economic constitutional order more than a single legislative enactment was called for. We had to build, you in the Congress and I, as the Executive, upon a broad base. Now, after thirty-four months of work, we contemplate a fairly rounded whole. We have returned the control of the Federal Government to the city of Washington.

Although liberals in and out of the government still had reservations about government restricting political freedoms, the distinction they were making between political and economic freedom was lost on the general public, as events were soon to prove.

With the onset of the cold war, the threat of subversion by the indigenous communists became one of our society's major concerns. What was more natural than that a people who had been exhorted to believe in government action for twenty years should see in government action the solution to this "new" major problem? If legislative investigations, however vigorous, were effective instruments for inquiring into business men's activities, then why should they not be equally good for inquiring into the communist problem? In this connection, a high percentage of the American people generally approved the controversial investigations being pursued by the late Senator McCarthy. If government action, however restrictive, was desirable in the economic sphere, why was it not equally desirable in the political realm? It is not necessary to deal with the substantive issues involved in these questions now. What is central to our discussion is the fact that the majority of the American people during the cold war were too willing to approve government action which restricted important liberties like free speech and press.

The recent American experience suggests two things. First, that if government intervention in the economic field is hailed as a virtue, there will be a tendency to so view it in the political area. Second, if there is validity to the distinction that liberals draw between political and economic freedom, the general public has failed to see it. It may be that the distinction is too subtle to be grasped by the electorate, and that a choice lies only between the alternatives of much government in both areas or little government in both areas.

Compatible Marriage: American Style

In view of the foregoing, it is clear that we in the United States have consummated a marriage between systems which are essentially compatible. More by trial and error than by design, we have achieved an economic system which fits the description disenchanted socialists now feel is the only one compatible with political democracy. We have "wide diffusion of property among individuals" and "effective profit-sharing." We have, too, the "indirect diffusion which goes with the growth of pension funds, workers' share banks, educational foundations, and charitable funds." We have in practice achieved the ideal set forth by Crosland: "a society in which ownership is thoroughly mixed-up—a society with a diverse, diffused, pluralist, and heterogeneous pattern of ownership, with the State, the nationalised industries, the Co-operatives, the Unions, Government financial pension funds, foundations, and millions of private families all participating." We have been able to prevent, as Crossman put it, "the concentration of power in the hands of *either* industrial management *or* the state bureaucracy—in brief, to distribute responsibility and so to enlarge freedom of choice."

To say that a marriage has been good is not to say that it has been perfect. We have had our troubles in the past, depressions, recessions, deprivations of liberty and the like. Nonetheless, the marriage between our political and economic systems has survived these troubles. Needless to say, there are crises ahead on which the marriage could founder. As a matter of fact, we already know what some of the major crises will be. For one, the cold war struggle must become more intense before it is resolved. Two, apparently, we are to have severe increases in unemployment as a consequence of automation. These problems undoubtedly will put some real strains on our political and economic systems. There will be many who will suggest that our present systems are no match for these problems. Whether the systems survive these crises will depend upon the faith, fortitude, and wisdom of the American people and their leaders. There is no inherent reason why these problems cannot be solved within the present framework.

WHICH ECONOMIC SYSTEM IS COMPATIBLE WITH POLITICAL AUTHORITARIANISM?

Authoritarians in control of governments have consistently recognized that it is crucial for them to control firmly the economies of their nations. The rationale offered for doing so is always couched in the most noble terms, i.e., for the good of the state. The basic idea in this rationale is that for the good of the nation there must be centralized control over every important aspect of life. As Mussolini put it:

Fascism conceives of the State as an absolute, in comparison with which all individuals or groups are relative, only to be conceived of in their relation to the State. . . .

For us Fascists, the State is not merely a guardian, preoccupied solely with the duty of assuring the personal safety of the citizens; nor is it an organization with purely material aims, such as to guarantee a certain level of well-being and peaceful conditions of life; for a mere council of administration would be sufficient to realize such objects. Nor is it a purely political creation, divorced from all contact with the complex material reality which makes up the life of the individual and the life of the people as a whole. The State, as conceived of and as created by Fascism, is a spiritual and moral fact in itself, since its political, juridical, and economic organization of the nation is a concrete thing: and such an organization must be in its origin and development a manifestation of the spirit.[9]

For Mussolini as for all authoritarians, lack of control by the government in important areas of the life of the people leads to destructive disunity: "When the conception of the State declines, and disunifying and centrifugal tendencies prevail, whether of individuals or of particular groups, the nations where such phenomena appear are in their decline."[10] This concept of the need for centralized control over all important aspects of life indicates why authoritarians traditionally cross swords with the Church. Obviously, it is a source of real concern to authoritarians that an agency

---

[9] Mussolini, *The Political and Social Doctrine of Fascism*, pp. 21–22.
[10] *Ibid.*, p. 22.

which they cannot control plays an important part in the lives of the people. Consequently, they have tried either to control the Church or to eliminate it as a real factor in the lives of the people.

Even as they attempt to centralize control, authoritarians cleverly impose their own special meaning upon words which have become meaningful to people everywhere. For example, like Mussolini, they try to show that only through centralization is "freedom" ever really achieved by the "individual":

Fascism desires the State to be a strong and organic body, at the same time reposing upon broad and popular support. The Fascist State has drawn into itself even the economic activities of the nation, and, through the corporative social and educational institutions created by it, its influence reaches every aspect of the national life and includes, framed in their respective organizations, all the political, economic and spiritual forces of the nation. A State which reposes upon the support of millions of individuals who recognize its authority, are continually conscious of its power and are ready at once to serve it, is not the old tyrannical State of the medieval lord nor has it anything in common with the absolute governments either before or after 1789. The individual in the Fascist State organizes the nation, but leaves a sufficient margin of liberty to the individual; the latter is deprived of all useless and possibly harmful freedom, but retains what is essential; the deciding power in this question cannot be the individual, but the State alone.[11]

Whatever the rationale, authoritarians have very real selfish reasons for maintaining a sure control over economic life. Were they to permit relative freedom in the economic sphere, concentrations of economic power in private hands would ultimately and surely develop. History teaches that economic power translates quickly into political power. Men representing concentrations of economic power will endeavor to use this power for political ends. If these political ends are not the same as those of the authoritarian government, the "disunifying and centrifugal tendencies" that Mussolini deprecated are set in motion and may ultimately threaten the political control of the authoritarians. Secondly, authoritarians are well-advised by history to be fearful of the contagion of ideas. If there is a wide latitude of freedom in the economic realm, people might carry over into their thinking on political arrangements ideas of freedom which would be anathema to authoritarianism.

On its face, it would appear that a government can achieve the

---

[11] *Ibid.*, p. 24.

maximum in control over the economy by owning it lock, stock, and barrel. Why, then have some authoritarian governments refrained from eliminating private property? When they did allow private ownership, how compatible were their economic and political systems?

The Relevant Experience of Nazism and Fascism

It is a matter of record that the nazis in Germany and the fascist authoritarians, Mussolini and Franco, did not nationalize their respective economies. It is clear, however in each case, that the government constantly expanded its control of the economy. In a unique way, the nazis did achieve a degree of "government ownership." The political leaders became owners of vast industrial empires. For example, Hermann Goering, one of Hitler's top aides, gradually built a structure of industrial properties which came to be known as the Hermann Goering Works. In Franco's Spain there are a substantial number of government-owned enterprises. But in the main, these authoritarians permitted private-ownership economies to exist, albeit under close government control. Why did they refrain from attempting government ownership? Apparently there are four leading reasons. First, the nazis and fascists did not believe that socialism was a practical solution in economics. As Rocco, the Italian fascist, wrote in 1925:

As for Socialism, the Fascist doctrine frankly recognizes that the problem raised by it as to the relations between capital and labor is a very serious one, perhaps the central one of modern life. What Fascism does not countenance is the collectivistic solution proposed by the Socialists. The chief defect of the socialistic method has been clearly demonstrated by the experience of the last few years. It does not take into account human nature, and is therefore outside reality, in that it will not recognize that the most powerful spring of human activities lies in individual self-interest and that therefore the elimination from the economic field of this interest results in complete paralysis. The suppression of private ownership of capital carries with it the suppression of capital itself, for capital is formed by the savings and no one will want to save, but will rather consume all he makes if he knows he cannot keep and hand down to his heirs the results of his labors. The dispersion of capital means the end of production since capital, no matter who owns it, is always an indispensible tool of production. Collective organization of production is followed therefore by the paralysis of production since, by eliminating from the productive mechanism the incentive of individual interest, the product becomes rarer and more costly. Socialism, then, as experience has shown, leads to increase in consumption, to the dispersion of capital and therefore to poverty. Of what avail is it, then, to build a social machine which will more justly distribute wealth if this very wealth is destroyed by construction of this machine? [12]

Secondly, each of these authoritarian regimes came to power in part because they opposed communism. In this connection, they had made special appeals to and derived help from those elements in their respective nations like big business which were violently opposed to government ownership, but who were less squeamish when it came to control with respect to political freedoms. Until such time as they felt secure in their power, they would, of course, be slow to adopt a program which was unpopular with elements which gave them support. Thirdly, for the government to take over the ownership of a going economy is a tremendous administrative effort. Former owners and managers who basically oppose government ownership cannot be relied upon to continue running their particular enterprises in the best interests of the new nationalization. It takes a great deal of time to train the new management group, as the Russians have learned. And since the nazis and fascists were preparing for war from the moment they came to power, they were not eager to embark on a program that might result in lowered production even for a temporary period. Lastly, since the fascism of Mussolini and the nazism of Hitler were relatively short-lived, we have no way of knowing what their final evolution might have been. We do know, however, that each of these regimes inexorably extended its control over the economy. All three ultimately reached the point where their control was so extensive as to be only a step away from the complete control which would have been theirs by government ownership. Nor was the fascism of Perón, based as it was on the support of working people, much different from the others in its application of power over the economy. And all of these regimes made it apparent in word and action that they felt threatened by the existence of concentrations of economic power which they did not control completely.

Compatible Marriage: Russian Style

The masters of Soviet communism from the beginning understood full well that they must control the economy just as firmly as they

---

[12] Rocco, *The Political Doctrine of Fascism*, pp. 21–22.

controlled the political apparatus. They recognized that concentration of economic power would threaten the authoritarian government. Unlike the nazis and fascists they were prepared both ideologically and practically to make a ruthless break with the past. As Stalin, explaining Lenin's views, put it:

It follows, first, that as long as we live in a small-peasant country, as long as we have not torn up the roots of capitalism, there is a surer economic basis for capitalism than for communism. It may happen that you cut down a tree but fail to tear up the roots; your strength does not suffice for this. Hence the *possibility* of the restoration of capitalism in our country.

Secondly, it follows that beside the possibility of the restoration of capitalism there is also the *possibility of the victory of socialism* [he is using socialism here as a synonym for communism] in our country, because we *can* remove the *possibility* of the restoration of capitalism, we can tear up the roots of capitalism and secure the final victory over capitalism, *if* we intensify the work of electrifying the country, *if* we place our industry, agriculture and transport on the technical basis of modern, large-scale industry. Hence the *possibility* of the victory of socialism in our country.[13]

The Russian leaders found that as a practical matter it was difficult to tear up the roots, particularly in the field of agriculture. But even though they made temporary concessions, they never lost sight of the need and goal of eliminating private ownership. According to Professor Merle Fainsod:

In its inception the Communist attitude toward the peasantry represented a curious combination of dependence and hostility. The dependence came from the necessity of appealing to the peasants' land-hunger in order to win and consolidate power in an overwhelmingly agrarian country. The hostility and distrust carried over as an ineluctable legacy from Marx, deriving from the conviction that the petty-bourgeois aspirations of the peasantry made it a natural enemy of any form of collectivism. In Lenin's words, "Small-scale production gives birth to capitalism and bourgeoisie constantly, daily, hourly, with elemental force, and in vast proportions." [14]

It is not surprising then, that Soviet leaders have moved as directly as they could and as ruthlessly as necessary to achieve complete dominion over the economy. At the conclusion of his fine study of the Soviet government Fainsod wrote:

[13] Stalin, *Leninism*, p. 81. [14] Fainsod, *How Russia Is Ruled*, p. 526.

There are some who argue that totalitarian dictatorship and a highly industrialized society are fundamentally incompatible, that the necessary result of industrialization is to pluralize authority among the functional groups created by it, that the diverse interests of these groups are likely to reflect themselves in the emergence of factions within the Communist Party, that these factions are likely to transcend the bounds of the Party and to take root in Soviet society, and that the end result of this process will be the emergence of some form of constitutional order which will make room for the legal interplay of parties and groups within the framework of a socialized economic order. While such a development would be warmly welcomed by all those who believe in the superior virtues of constitutional systems, the probability that it will soon take place does not appear great.

Both the doctrines and practice of Bolshevism militate against such a trend. A Party leadership which bases its authority on the suppression of factions is hardly likely to accede to a course of development which produces splits in its ranks and loss of its monopoly of power. There is danger too in being unduly beguiled by that special variety of technological determinism which assumes that those who possess important skills in a society inevitably transmute such skills into political power. There is no iron law which prevents dictators from presiding over the destinies of highly industrialized societies.

This does not mean that the Communist Party leadership may not find it desirable to make continuous readjustments in its methods of rule to take account of the increasing complexities of managing an industrialized society. It already insists that the Party cadres to whom it entrusts control functions must possess a degree of technological and managerial sophistication adequate to cope with their coordinating and supervisory responsibilities. Experimentation is likely to continue in the search for a proper balance between central Party controls and delegations of operational authority calculated to stimulate local initiative and to increase efficiency. The Party leadership will undoubtedly persist in putting a special premium on the complex of skills so essential to industrialization. But though it counts heavily on the contributions of its industrial elite and rewards its members accordingly, it is highly unlikely to permit them to emerge as autonomous power groups, and even tentative moves in this direction are likely to be nipped in the bud. *The first law of the Party leadership is its own self-preservation; it can be expected to take the sternest measures to prevent any encroachment on its own supreme authority* [15] [italics supplied].

In short, the masters of the Soviet Union are aware that the only way to maintain sure control politically is to hold the power to

---

[15] *Ibid.*, p. 592.

control every aspect of life in the Soviet Union. However much we may deprecate Russian totalitarianism, we must admit that the Soviets have consummated a compatible marriage. A government-owned and controlled economy makes the best partner for an authoritarian political system.

DOES IT MATTER WHICH PARTNER IS DOMINANT?

In discussing the issues raised here, we have placed emphasis first on the political systems. We raised the question of compatibility in these terms: which economic system is compatible with democratic government? It is natural, of course, to ask, what happens where the people of a particular society or its leadership put primary emphasis on the economic systems? Certainly, it is true that some people would urge that a government-ownership economy is the most desirable achievement and that we should start with this in mind and try to seek out the answer to the question of compatibility in these terms: which government is most compatible with such an economy? Actually, the result would be the same whichever way the question is raised. For the question of compatibility is answered by matching the characteristics of the systems to see which apparently square best with one another. Starting with the economic systems as a base and seeking the political systems which are most compatible with them would net the same results as our inquiry, which places primary emphasis on the political systems.

SELECTED BIBLIOGRAPHY

C. A. R. CROSLAND, *The Conservative Enemy* (New York: Schocken Books, Inc., 1962).

C. A. R. CROSLAND, *The Future of Socialism* (London: Jonathan Cape, 1956).

R. H. S. CROSSMAN (ed.), *New Fabian Essays* (London: Turnstile Press, 1952).

MERLE FAINSOD, *How Russia Is Ruled* (Cambridge: Harvard University Press, 1963).

A LAST WORD

If the foregoing analysis makes sense, the reasons for the strength, vitality, and virtue of the marriage of democracy and capitalism are readily apparent. Each system in its own sphere comes much closer to fulfilling the universal aspirations for government and the economy than the alternatives available. Each is predicated on a realistic appraisal of human nature and human needs and responds better to them than the alternatives. Based upon the same kind of appeals and needs, the systems are compatible. This is in and of itself a source of strength. But, more important, each reinforces the strength of the other, giving the marriage the value of a sum greater than one plus one.

Proponents of democratic-capitalism must bear in mind that, despite its virtue, there are always those, even in societies in which it prevails, who do not believe in it and seek to destroy it. There is no reason to believe that democratic-capitalism will automatically survive or prevail. To maintain it and make it work well requires understanding and effort on the part of the great majority of the people in the society. This is not to suggest that the democracy and capitalism of the 1960's must remain unchanged as to specifics. That would be as undesirable as it is impossible. Rather, it is to suggest that we seek to maintain the fundamental bases of the system even as we modify the specifics to meet changing times. It behooves citizens of a country like the United States to examine thoroughly its institutions so as to appreciate their strengths and weaknesses and to seek to maintain their essence even while trying to improve them.

The words uttered by John Philpot Curran, Irish patriot of the late eighteenth and early nineteenth centuries, still have relevance:

It is the common fate of the indolent to see their rights become a prey to the active. The condition upon which God hath given liberty to man is eternal vigilance; which condition if he break, servitude is at once the consequence of this crime and the punishment of his guilt.

INDEX